Griffin's

Easy to Pronounce

French

by
Cliff Davis

Griffin Publishing
Glendale, California

10 9 8 7 6 5 4 3 2

ISBN 1-882180-22-4

Griffin Publishing
544 Colorado Street
Glendale, California 91204

Telephone: 1-800-423-5789

Manufactured in the United States of America

INTRODUCTION

The EASY TO PRONOUNCE phrase book series has been developed with the conviction that learning to speak a foreign language should be fun and easy.

The EPLS Vowel Symbols is a unique phonetic system that stresses consistency , clarity and above all, simplicity! The basic Vowel Symbols have been placed on the back cover for easy reference.

You will be amazed at how confidence in your pronunciation will lead to an eagerness to talk to other people in their own language.

ACKNOWLEDGMENTS

The EASY TO PRONOUNCE LANGUAGE SYSTEM (EPLS) has been developed by Cliff Davis.

Series Editor
Richard D. Burns, Ph.D.

Series Associate Editor
Mark M. Dodge, M.A.

French Language Consulting Editor
Dave Miller

Book Design and Typeset
Regina Books, Claremont California.

Cover Design
Sylvia Hoffland, Long Beach, California.

Reviewers
Carol Ann J. Fuller; Paul M. Richins, Bob Levis

This book is dedicated to
Betty Chapman
with special thanks to
Priscilla Leal Bailey

CONTENTS

PRONUNCIATION GUIDE

Most English speakers are familiar with the French word **merci**. This is how its correct pronunciation would be represented in this system.

M©ÊR-S℗℗

All French vowel sounds are assigned a specific non changing symbol. When these symbols are used in conjunction with consonants and read normally, pronunciation of even the most difficult foreign word becomes incredibly EASY.

On the following page you find all the symbols used in this book. They are EASY to LEARN since their sounds are familiar. Beneath each symbol are three English words which contain the sound of the symbol.

THE SAME BASIC SYMBOLS ARE USED IN ALL EASY TO PRONOUNCE PHRASE BOOKS!

EPLS VOWEL SYMBOLS

(A)

Ace
Bake
Safe

(EE)

See
Green
Feet

(O)

Oak
Cold
Phone

(oo)

Cool
Pool
Too

(ă)

Cat
Sad
Hat

(ĕ)

Men
Red
Bed

(ah)

Rock
Hot
Off

(uh)

Up
Sun
Run

(ew)

New
Few
Dew

This symbol represents the French letter **u**. Put your lips together as if to kiss and say EE.

(ou)

Could
Would
Cook

This symbol represents a unique sound found in the letters **eu** in French spelling...To master this sound you must listen to a native speaker's pronunciation. The **ou** sound in **could** is an effective substitute.

NASALIZED VOWEL SOUNDS

In French certain vowels are nasalized. This (ñ) immediately following a symbol tells you to nasalize the sound that the symbol represents. Try pinching your nose while pronouncing these words: (try not to sound the n in the words)

can	zone	on	sun
(ā)ñ	(O)ñ	(ah)ñ	(uh)ñ

EPLS CONSONANTS

Consonants are letters like **T**, **D**, and **K**. They are easy to recognize and their pronunciation seldom changes. The following pronunciation guide letters represent some unique French consonant sounds.

R   represents the French **r**. Try to pronounce it far back in the throat. Listen to a native speaker to master this sound.

ZH   pronounce these guide letters like the **s** in measure.

KW   like the **qu** in **qu**it

PRONUNCIATION TIPS

- Each pronunciation guide word is broken into syllables. Read each word slowly, one syllable at a time, increasing speed as you become more familiar with the system.

- In general, equal emphasis is given to each syllable. Sometimes the French will slightly stress the last syllable in a word.

- Most of the symbols are pronounced the way they look!

- This phrase book provides a means to speak and be understood in French. To perfect your French accent you must listen closely to French speakers and adjust your speech accordingly.

- Some pronunciation guide letters are underlined.(**Z T N**) This is simply to let you know that the underlined letter is a linking sound which appears to separate two vowel sounds.

- **SVP** is the abbreviation for **s'il vous plait** which means please. You will see it througout the book.

ESSENTIAL WORDS AND PHRASES

Here are some basic words and phrases that will help you express your needs and feelings in French.

Hello
Bonjour

BOñ ZHOOR

How are you?
Comment allez-vous?

KO-MOñ Tah-LA-Voo

Fine/ Very well
Très bien

TRA BEE-añ

And you?
Et vous?

A Voo

Goodbye
Au revoir

O Ruh-VWah R

Good morning

Bonjour

BONñ ZHOOR

Good evening

Bon soir

BONñ SWahR

Good night

Bonne nuit

BuhN NWEE

Mr.

Monsieur

Muh-SYou

Mrs.

Madame

Mah-DahM

Miss

Mademoiselle

MahD-MWah-ZěL

Yes
Oui

WEE

No
Non

NOñ

Please
S'il vous plaît

SEEL VOO PLĕ

Abbreviated SVP throughout book

Thank you
Merci

MĕR-SEE

Excuse me
Pardon

PahR-DOñ

I'm sorry
Je suis désolé

ZHuh SWEE DA-SO-LA

I'm a tourist

Je suis touriste

ZH⒰ SW⒠ T⒪-R⒠ST

I don't speak French

Je ne parle pas français.

ZH⒰N-⒰ P⒜RL P⒜ FR⒜ñ-S⒜

I speak a little French

Je parle un peu francais

ZH⒰ P⒜RL ⒰ñ P⒪

FR⒜ñ-S⒜

Do you understand English?

Comprenez-vous anglais?

K⒪ñ-PR⒰-N⒜ V⒪ ⒜ñ-GL⒜

I don't understand!

Je ne comprends pas!

ZH⒰N-⒰ K⒪ñ-PR⒜ñ P⒜

Please repeat

Répétez s'il vous plaît

R⒜-P⒜-T⒜ SVP

I want...

Je veux...

ZH(uh) V(ou)...

I have...

J'ai......

ZH(A)...

I know

Je sais

ZH(uh) S(A)

I don't know

Je ne sais pas

ZH(uh)N S(A) P(ah)

I like it

Je l'aime bien

ZH(uh) L(ĕ)M B(EE)-(ã)ñ

I don't like it

Je ne l'aime pas bien

ZH(uh)N-(uh) L(ĕ)M P(ah) B(EE)-(ã)ñ

I am...

Je suis...

ZH(uh) SW(EE)...

I'm lost

Je suis perdu

ZH(uh) SW(EE) P(ĕ)R-D(ew)

I'm in a hurry

Je suis pressé

ZH(uh) SW(EE) PR(ĕ)-S(A)

I'm tired

Je suis fatigué

ZH(uh) SW(EE) F(ah)-T(EE)-G(A)

I'm ill

Je suis malade

ZH(uh) SW(EE) M(ah)-L(ah)D

I'm hungry

J'ai faim

ZH(A) F(ã)ñ

I'm thirsty

J'ai soif

ZH(A) SW(ah)F

I'm angry

Je suis en colère

ZH(uh) SW(EE) Z(ah)ñ K(O)-L(ĕ)R

My name is...

Je m'appelle...

ZH⑩ M⑨-P⑥L...

What's your name?

Comment vous appelez-vous?

K⑩-M⑩ñ V⑩ Z⑨-PL⑨ V⑩

Where are you from?

D'où venez-vous?

D⑩ V⑩-N⑨ V⑩

Do you live here?

Habitez -vous ici?

⑨-B⑥-T⑨ V⑩ Z⑥-S⑥

I just arrived

Je viens d'arriver

ZH⑩ V⑥-⑨ñ D⑨-R⑥-V⑨

What hotel are you [staying] at?

Vous restez à quel hôtel?

V⑩ R⑥S-T⑨ ⑨ K⑥ L⑩-T⑥L

I'm at the...hotel

Je reste à l'hôtel....

ZH⑩ R⑥ST ⑨ L⑩-T⑥L...

It was nice to meet you

Je suis enchanté de faire votre connaissance

ZH(uh)   SW(EE)   Z(ah)ñ-SH(ah)ñ-T(A)
D(uh)   F(ěR   V(O)-TR(uh)
K(O)-N(A)-S(ah)ñS

See you tomorrow

A demain

(ah)   D(uh)-M(ā)ñ

See you later

A bientôt

(ah)   B(EE)-(ā)ñ-T(O)

So long!

A tout à l'heure!

(ah)   T(oo)T   (ah)   L(ou)R

Good luck!

Bonne chance!

B(uh)N   SH(ah)ñS

In this book the symbol (uh) is used to represent the French letter **e** in words such as le, de , etc. To master your French accent have a French speaker pronounce these words and try to hone your accent accordingly.

THE BIG QUESTIONS

Who?

Qui?

K

Who is it?

Qui est -ce?

KⒺⒺ　ⓔS

What?

Quoi?　　　　　Comment?

KWⓐⓗ　　　KⓄ-MⓄñ

What's that?

Qu'est-ce que c'est?

KⓔS-Kⓤⓗ　SⒶ

When?

Quand?

Kⓐⓗñ

Where?

Où?

Where is...?

Où est...?

 A...

Which?

Quel?   Quelle?   Quels?   Quelles?

KĕL

Although spelled differently these are all pronounced the same.

Why?

Pourquoi?

PⓄR KWⓐh

How?

Comment?

KⓄ-MⓄñ

How much? (money)

Combien?

KⓄñ-BEE-ⓐñ

How long?

Combien de temps?

KⓄñ-BEE-ⓐñ Dⓤh Tⓐhñ

ASKING FOR THINGS

The following phrases are valuable when asking for directions, food or help, etc.

I would like...

Je voudrais...

ZH⓾ V⓪-DR④...

I need...

J'ai besoin...

ZH④ B⓾-ZW④ñ...

Can you...

Pouvez-vous...

P⓪-V④-V⓪...

When asking for things be sure to say

please and thank you

Please

S'il vous plait

SⓔⓔL V⓪ PL⓮

Thank you

Merci

M⓮R-Sⓔⓔ

PHRASEMAKER

Combine **I would like** with the following phrases beneath it and you will have a good idea how to ask for things.

I would like...

Je voudrais...

↓ ZH⓿ V⓿-DR⒜...

more coffee

plus de café

PL⓿ D⓿ K⒜-F⒜

some water

de l'eau

D⓿ L⓿

some ice

de la glace

D⓿ L⒜ GL⒜S

the menu

la menu

L⓿ Mⓔ-N⓿

PHRASEMAKER

Here are a few sentences you can use when you feel the urge to say **I need**...or **can you**?

I need...

J'ai besoin...

ZH④ B⑩-ZW④ñ...

---

help

d'aide

D⑥D

---

directions

de directions

D⑩ D㊙-R⑥K-S㊙-◎ñ

---

more money

de plus d'argent

D⑩ PL⑩ D⑩R-ZH⑩ñ

---

change

de monnaie

D⑩ M◎-N④

---

a lawyer

d'un avocat

D⑩ñ N⑩-V◎-K⑩

Can you...

Pouvez-vous...

↓ P◉◉-V◈-V◉◉...

---

help me?

m'aider?

M◈-D◈

---

show me?

me montrer?

M◉ M◉ñ-TR◈

---

give me...?

me donner...?

M◉ D◉-N◈...

---

tell me...?

me dire...?

M◉ D◉R...

---

take me to...?

m'emmener...?

M◉M-N◈...

ASKING THE WAY

No matter how independent you are, sooner or later you'll probably have to ask directions.

Where is...?

Où est...?

OO A...

Is it near?

C'est près d'ici?

SA PRA DEE-SEE

Is it far?

C'est loin d'ici?

SA LWañ DEE-SEE

I'm lost!

Je suis perdu!

ZHuh SWEE PëR-Dew

I'm looking for...

Je cherche...

ZHuh SHëRSH...

PHRASEMAKER

Where is...

Où est...

the restroom?

la toilette?

the telephone?

le téléphone?

the beach?

la plage?

the hotel...?

l'hôtel...?

LO-TĕL...

the train for...?

le train à...?

TIME

What time is it?

Quelle heure est-il?

K ⓔ L ⓞⓤR Ⓐ-T ⓔⓔL

Morning

Le matin

L ⓤⓗ M ⓐⓗ-T ⓐ ñ

Noon

Midi

M ⓔⓔ-D ⓔⓔ

Night

La nuit

L ⓐⓗ NW ⓔⓔ

Today

Aujourd'hui

Ⓞ-ZH ⓞⓞR-DW ⓔⓔ

Tomorrow

Demain

D ⓤⓗ-M ⓐ ñ

This week
Cette semaine

SēT Suh-MēN

This month
Ce mois

Suh MWah

This year
Cette année

SēT ah-NA

Now
Maintenant

Mañ-Tuh-Nahñ

Soon
Bientôt

BEE-añ-TO

Later
Plus tard

PLew TahR

Never
Jamais

ZHah-MA

WHO IS IT?

I

Je

ZH⓾

You (Formal)	**(Informal)**
Vous	Tu
V⓿	T⓮
Use this form of you with people you don't know well	Use this form of you with people you know well

We

Nous

N⓿

They	
Ils (m)	Elles (f)
ⓔⒺL	ⓔL
A group of men only or a group of men & women	A group of women only

THE, A (AN), AND SOME

To use the correct form of The, A (An), or Some, you must know if the French word is masculine or feminine. Often you will have to guess! If you make a mistake, you will still be understood.

The

La	Les
L(ah)	L(A)
The before a singular feminine noun (La) woman is pretty	**The** before a plural feminine noun (Les) women are pretty
Le	Les
L(uh)	L(A)
The before a singular masculine noun (Le) man is handsome	**The** before a plural masculine noun (Les) men are handsome

A or An

Un	Une
(uh)ñ	(ew)N
A or **an** before a singular masculine noun He is (un) man	**A** or **an** before a singular feminine noun She is (une) woman

Some

Du	De la
D(ew)	D(uh) L(ah)
Some before singular masculine nouns (Du) men	**Some** before singular feminine nouns (De la) women

USEFUL OPPOSITES

Near	**Far**
Près	Loin
PR④	LW④ñ

Here	**There**
Ici	Là
⑥-S⑥	L⑨

Left	**Right**
A gauche	A droite
⑨ G◉SH	⑨ DRW⑨T

A little	**A lot**
Un peu	Beaucoup
⑩ñ P◉	B◉-K◉

More	**Less**
Plus	Moins
PL⑥	MW④ñ

Big	**Small**
Grand (m), Grande (f)	Petit (m), Petite (f)
GR⑨ñ, GR⑨ND	P⑩-T⑥, P⑩-T⑥T

In French adjectives are masculine or feminine depending on the noun they describe.

Opened

Ouvert (m), Ouverte (f)

oo-VẽR, oo-VẽRT

Closed

Fermé (m), Fermée (f)

FẽR-MA

Cheap

Bon marché

BOñ Mah-R-SHA

Expensive

Cher (m), Chère (f)

SHẽR

Clean

Propre

PRO-PRuh

Dirty

Sale

Sah-L

Good

Bon (m), Bonne (f)

BOñ, Buh-N

Bad

Mauvais (m), Mauvaise (f)

MO-VA, MO-VẽZ

Vacant

Libre

LEE-BRuh

Occupied

Occupé (m), Occupée (f)

O-Koo-PA

Right

Avoir raison

ah-VWah-R RA-ZOñ

Wrong

Avoir tort

ah-VWah-R TOR

WORDS OF ENDEARMENT

I love you
Je t'aime

ZH(uh) T(ē)M

My love
Mon amour

M(O)ñ N(ah)-M(oo)R

My life
Ma vie

M(ah) V(EE)

My friend (to a male)
Mon ami (m)

M(O)ñ N(ah)-M(EE)

My friend (to a female)
Mon amie (f)

M(O)ñ N(ah)-M(EE)

Kiss me!
Embrassez-moi!

(ah)ñ-BR(ah)-S(A) MW(ah)

WORDS OF ANGER

What do you want?

Qu'est-ce que vous voulez?

K(ẽ)S K(uh) V(oo) V(oo)-L(A)

Leave me alone!

Laissez-moi tranquille!

L(A)-S(A) MW(ah) TR(ah)ñ-K(ee)L

Go away!

Allez-vous-en!

(ah)-L(A) V(oo)-Z(ah)ñ

Stop bothering me!

Ne me dérangez pas!

N(uh) M(uh) D(A)-R(ah)ñ-ZH(A) P(ah)

Be Quiet!

Taisez-vous!

T(A)-Z(A) V(oo)

That's enough!

C'est assez!

S(A) T(ah)-S(A)

COMMON EXPRESSIONS

When you are at a loss for words but have the feeling you should say something, try one of these!

Who knows?

Qui sait?

K⒠ S⒜

That's the truth!

C'est la vérité!

S⒜ L⒜ⁿ V⒜-R⒠-T⒜

Sure!

Bien sûr!

B⒠-⒜ñ S⒠wR

Wow!

Chouette!

SH⒪-⒠T

What's happening?

Qu'est-ce qui se passe?

K⒠S K⒠ S⒰ P⒜S

I think so!

Je pense que oui!

ZH⒰ P⒜ñS K⒰ W⒠

Cheers!

A votre santé!

 VO-TR(uh) S(ah)ñ-T(A)

Good luck!

Bonne chance!

B(uh)N SH(ah)ñS

With pleasure!

Avec plaisir!

(ah)-V(e)K PL(A)-Z(EE)R

My goodness!

Mon dieu!

M(O)ñ DY(ou)

What a shame or Thats too bad!

C'est dommage!

S(A) D(O)-M(ah)ZH

Well done! Bravo!

Bravo!

BR(ah)-V(O)

Never mind!

N'importe quoi!

N(ã)ñ-P(O)RT KW(ah)

USEFUL COMMANDS

Stop!
Arrêtez!

ah-Rĕ-TA

Go!
Allez!

ah-LA

Wait!
Attendez!

ah-Tahñ-DA

Hurry!
Dépêchez-vous!

DA-Pĕ-SHA Voo

Slow down!
Lentement!

Lahñ-Tuh-Mahñ

Come here!
Venez ici!

Vuh-NA ZEE-SEE

Help!
Au secours!

O Suh-KooR

EMERGENCIES

Fire!

Au feu!

Ⓞ Fⓞⓤ

Emergency!

L'urgence!

LⓞⓤR-ZHⓐⓗñS

Call the police!

Téléphonez au police!

Tⓐ-Lⓐ-Fⓞ-Nⓐ Ⓞ Pⓞ-LⒺⒺS

Call a doctor!

Téléphonez au médecin!

Tⓐ-Lⓐ-Fⓞ-Nⓐ Ⓞ Mⓐ-Dⓤⓗ-Sⓐñ

Call an ambulance!

Faites venir une ambulance!

FⒺT Vⓤⓗ-NⒺⒺR ⓔⓦN
ⓐⓗñ-Bⓔⓦ-LⓐⓗñS

I need help

Au secours!

Ⓞ Sⓤⓗ-KⓞⓞR

ARRIVAL

Passing through customs should be easy since there are usually agents available who speak English. You may be asked how long you intend to stay and if you have anything to declare.

- Have your passport ready.

- Be sure all documents are up to date.

- While in a foreign country, it is wise to keep receipts for everything you buy.

- Be aware that many countries will charge a departure tax when you leave. Your travel agent should be able to find out if this affects you.

- If you have connecting flights, be sure to reconfirm them in advance.

- Make sure your luggage is clearly marked inside and out.

- Take valuables and medicines in carry on bags.

SIGNS TO LOOK FOR:

DOUANE (CUSTOMS)
FRONTIERE (BORDER)
LES BAGAGES (BAGGAGE CLAIM)

KEY WORDS

Baggage
Les bagages

L@ B@-G@ZH

Customs
La douane

L@ DW@N

Documents
Les documents

L@ D@-K@-M@ñ

Passport
Le passeport

L@ P@S-P@R

Porter
Le porteur

L@ P@R-T@R

Tax
La taxe

L@ T@KS

USEFUL PHRASES

I have nothing to declare

Je n'ai rien à déclarer

ZH⒰ N⒜ R㋣-⒜ñ ⒜h
D⒜-KL⒜-R⒜

I'll be staying...

Je vais rester...

↓ ZH⒰ V⒜ R㋤S-T⒜...

one week

une semaine

⒠wN S⒰-M㋤N

two weeks

deux semaines

D⒪ S⒰-M㋤N

one month

un mois

⒰ñ MW⒜h

two months

deux mois

D⒪ MW⒜h

I'm here on business

Je suis en voyage d'affaires

ZH(uh) SW(EE) Z(ah)ñ VW(ah)-Y(ah)ZH D(ah)-F(ĕ)R

I'm here on vacation

Je suis en vacances

ZH(uh) SW(EE) Z(ah)ñ V(ah)-K(ah)ñS

Here is my passport

Voici mon passeport

VW(ah)-S(EE) M(O)ñ P(ah)S-P(O)R

Is there a problem?

Il y a un problème?

(EE)L (EE) (ah) (uh)ñ PR(O)-BL(ĕ)M

I don't understand!

Je ne comprends pas!

ZH(uh)N-(uh) K(O)ñ-PR(ah)ñ P(ah)

Do you speak English?

Parlez-vous anglais?

P(ah)R-L(A) V(oo) Z(ah)ñ-GL(A)

PHRASEMAKER

Where is...

Ou est...

...

customs?

La douane

L⒜ DW⒜N

baggage claim?

le depot de bagages?

L⒰ D⒜-P⒪ D⒰ B⒜-G⒜ZH

the money exchange?

le bureau d'échange?

L⒰ B⒠W-R⒪ D⒜-SH⒜ñZH

the taxi stand?

la station de taxi?

L⒜ ST⒜-S⒠⒠-⒪ñ D⒰ T⒜K-S⒠⒠

the bus stop?

Où est l'arrêt d'autobus?

I need a porter!

Jai besoin de porteur!

ZHⒶ Bⓗ-ZWãñ Dⓗ PⓈR-TⓈR

These are my bags

Voici mes bagages

VWⓑ-SⒶⒶ MⒶ Bⓑ-GⓑZH

I'm missing a bag

Je manque une valise

ZHⓗ Mⓑñ KⒶN Vⓑ-LⒶⒶS

Take my bags to a taxi please

Prenez mes valises au taxi s'il vous plaît

PRⓗ-NⒶ MⒶ Vⓑ-LⒶⒶS Ⓢ

TⓑK-SⒶⒶ SVP

Thank you. This is for you

Merci. C'est pour vous

MⒶR-SⒶⒶ SⒶ PⓈR Vⓒ

HOTEL SURVIVAL

A wide selectiion of accommodations, ranging from the most basic to the most extravagant, are available wherever you travel in France. When booking your room, find out what amenities are included for the price you pay.

- Make reservations well in advance and get written confirmation of reservation before you leave home.

- Always have identification ready when checking in.

- Hotels in some foreign countries may require you to hand over your passport when checking in. It is usually returned the next day.

- Do not leave valuables, prescriptions or cash in your room when you are not there!

- Electrical items like blow dryers may need an adaptor. Your hotel may be able to provide one, but to be safe take one with you.

- "SERVICE COMPRIS" or "TOUTES TAXES COMPRISES" on your bill means tip is already included except for bellman.

KEY WORDS

Hotel

l'hôtel

LO-TёL

Bellman

Un garçon d'hôtel

uhñ GahR-SOñ DO-TёL

Maid

Une domestique

ewN DO-MёS-TEEK

Message

Le message

Luh MёS-SahZH

Reservation

La réservation

Lah RA-SёR-Vah-SEE-Oñ

Room service

Service dans les chambres

SёR-VEES Dah LA SHahñ-BRuh

CHECKING IN

My name is...

Je m'appelle...

ZHuh Mah-PĕL...

I have a reservation

J'ai réservé

ZHA RA-SĕR-VA

Have you any vacancies?

Vous avez des chambres libres?

Voo Zah-VA DA SHahñ-BRuh LEE-BRuh

What is the charge?

Quel est le prix?

Kĕ LA Luh PREE

Is there room service?

Il y a la service dans les chambres?

EEL EE ah Lah SĕR-VEES Dahñ LA SHahñ-BRuh

I would like a room...

Je voudrais une chambre ...

ZH(uh) V(oo)-DR(a) (ew)N

↓SH(a)ñ-BR(uh)...

with a bath

avec une salle de bains

(ah)-V(e)K (ew)N S(ah)L D(uh) B(a)ñ

with a shower

avec une douche

(ah)-V(e)K (ew)N D(oo)SH

with one bed

à un lit

(ah) (uh)ñ L(EE)

with two beds

à deux lits

(ah) D(ou) L(EE)

with a view

avec la vue

(ah)-V(e)K L(ah) V(ew)

USEFUL PHRASES

Where is the dining room?

Où est la salle à manger?

ⓞⓞ　Ⓐ　Lⓐh　SⓐhL　ⓐh　Mⓐhñ-ZHⒶ

Are meals included?

Est-ce que les repas sont compris?

ⓔS-Kⓤh　LⒶ　Rⓤh-Pⓐh

SⓄñ　KⓄñ-PRⒺ

What time is...

A quelle heure est...

⬇ ⓐh　Kⓔ　LⓞⓤR　Ⓐ...

breakfast?

le petit déjeuner?

Lⓤh　Pⓤh-TⒺ　DⒶ-ZHⓞⓤ-N�Ⓐ

lunch?

le déjeuner?

Lⓤh　DⒶ-ZHⓞⓤ-NⒶ

dinner?

le dîner?

Lⓤh　DⒺ-NⒶ

My room key please

Ma clé de chambre s'il vous plaît

M(ah) KL(A) D(uh) SH(ah)ñ-BR(uh) SVP

Are there any messages for me?

Y a-t-il des messages pour moi?

(EE) (ah) T(EE)L D(A) M(ĕ)-S(ah)ZH
P(oo)R MW(ah)

Please wake me at...

Veuillez me réveiller à...

↓V(ou)-Y(A) M(uh) R(A)-V(A)-Y(A) (ah)...

6:00

six heures

S(EE) Z(ou)R

6:30

six heures et demie

S(EE) Z(ou)R Z(A) D(uh)-M(EE)

7:00

sept heures

S(ĕ) T(ou)R

7:30

sept heures et demie

S(ĕ) T(ou)R Z(A) D(uh)-M(EE)

8:00

huit heures

W(EE) T(ou)R

8:30

huit heures et demie

W(EE) T(ou)R Z(A) D(uh)-M(EE)

9:00

neuf heures

N(ou) V(ou)R

9:30

neuf heures et demie

N(ou) V(ou)R Z(A) D(uh)-M(EE)

PHRASEMAKER

I need...

J'ai besoin...

↓ ZH④ B⑩-ZW③ñ...

soap

de savon

D⑩ S⑧-V⓪ñ

more towels

de plus de serviettes

D⑩ PL⑩ D⑩ S⑧R-V⑪-⑧T

ice cubes

de glaçons

D⑩ GL⑧-S⓪ñ

toilet paper

de papier hygiénique

D⑩ P⑧-P⑪-④ ⑪-ZH⑪-④-N⑪K

a bellman

d'un garçon d'hôtel

D⑩ñ G⑧R-S⓪ñ D⓪-T⑧L

↓

a maid

de domestique

D(uh) DO-M(e)S-T(EE)K

the manager

de directeur (m)   De directrice (f)

D(uh) D(EE)-R(e)K-T(oo)R   D(uh) D(EE)-R(e)K-TR(EE)S

a babysitter

d'une garde-bébé

D(ew)N G(ah)RD B(A)-B(A)

an extra key

d'un clé supplémentaire

D(uh)ñ KL(A) S(ew)-PL(A)-M(uh)ñ-T(e)R

a hotel safe

d'un coffre-fort

D(uh)ñ KO-FR(uh) F(O)R

clean sheets

les draps propres

L(A) DR(ah)P PR(O)-PR(uh)

more blankets

de plus de couvertures

D(uh) PL(ew) D(uh) K(oo)-V(e)R-T(ew)R

PHRASEMAKER
(PROBLEMS)

There is no...

Il n'y a pas...

ⓔL NYⓐ Pⓐ...

hot water

d'eau chaude

Dⓞ SHⓞD

heat

de chauffage

Dⓤⓗ SHⓞ-Fⓐ ZH

light

de lumière

Dⓤⓗ LⓞⓞM-Yⓔ R

electricity

d'électricité

Dⓐ Lⓔ K-TRⓔⓔ-Sⓔⓔ-Tⓐ

toilet paper

de papier hygiénique

Dⓤⓗ Pⓐ-Pⓔⓔ-ⓐ ⓔⓔ-ZHⓔⓔ-ⓐ-NⓔⓔK

PHRASEMAKER
(SPECIAL NEEDS)

Do you have...

Avez-vous...

 ⓐ-Vⓐ Vⓞⓞ...

facilities for the disabled?

des aménagements pour les handicapes?

Dⓐ Zⓐ-Mⓐ-NⓐZH-Mⓐñ PⓞⓞR
Lⓐ Hⓐ N-Dⓔⓔ-Kⓐ P

a wheel chair?

un fauteuils roulants?

ⓤñ Fⓞ-Tⓞⓤ-Yⓤ Rⓞⓞ-Lⓐñ

an elevator?

un ascenseur?

ⓤñ Nⓐ-Sⓐñ-SⓞⓤR

a ramp?

une rampe?

ⓔⓦN Rⓐ MP

CHECKING OUT

The bill please

Voulez-vous me préparer la note s'il vous plaît?

V⊙⊙-L▲ V⊙⊙ M⊙h PR▲-P⊙h-R▲
L⊙h N⊙T SVP

Is this bill correct?

Il y a une erreur dans la note?

⒠L ⒠ ⊙h ⊙wN ⒠R-⊙⊙R
D⊙hñ L⊙h N⊙T

Do you accept credit cards?

Acceptez-vous les cartes de crédit?

⊙h-S⒠P-T▲ V⊙⊙ L▲ K⊙hRT
D⊙h KR▲-D⒠

Could you have my luggage brought down?

Pouvez-vous faire descendre mes bagages?

P⊙⊙-V▲-V⊙⊙ F⒠R D▲-S⊙hñ-DR⊙h
M▲ B⊙h-G⊙hZH

Can you call a taxi for me?

Appelez-moi un taxi s'il vous plaît?

ah-PLA MWah uhñ TahK-SEE SVP

I had a very good time!

Je me suis bien amusé!

ZHuh Muh SWEE BEE-añ
Nah-Mew-ZA

Thanks for everything

Merci pour tout

MeR-SEE PooR Too

I'll see you next time

A la prochaine

ah Lah PRO-SHaN

Goodbye

Au revoir

O Ruh-VWahR

RESTAURANT SURVIVAL

From sidewalk cafés to the most elegant restaurants, you will find a delectable assortment of French cuisine.

- Breakfast (le petit déjeuner) is usually small, served at your hotel. Lunch (le dejuner) is normally served from 12:30 to 3 p.m. Dinner (le dîner) begins at 8 p.m. and can extend for hours. It is more formal than lunch and a time for enjoyment of great French cuisine and wine!

- Menus are posted outside eating establishments and may contain the following statements; (**Service Comprls**) or (**Prix Nets**) service included, (**Non Compris**) service not included.

SIGNS TO LOOK FOR:

AUBERGE   (COUNTRY INN)

BISTRO (SIMILAR TO A PUB OR TAVERN)

CAFE (CAFE)

CREPERIE (CREPE SHOP)

RESTAURANT (TRADITIONAL)

KEY WORDS

Breakfast

le petit déjeuner

L⬤uh P⬤uh-T⬤EE D⬤A-ZH⬤ou-N⬤A

Lunch

le déjeuner

L⬤uh D⬤A-ZH⬤ou-N⬤A

Dinner

le dîner

L⬤uh D⬤EE-N⬤A

Waiter

le garçon

L⬤uh G⬤ah R-S⬤O ñ

Waitress

la serveuse

L⬤ah S⬤ẽ R-V⬤ou S

Restaurant

le restaurant

L⬤uh R⬤ẽ S-T⬤O-R⬤ah ñ

USEFUL PHRASES

A table for...

Une table à...

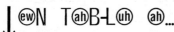

2	4	6
deux	quatre	six

The menu please

La carte s'il vous plaît

L@ K@RT SVP

Separate checks please

L'addition individuelle s'il vous plaît

L@-D©-S©-Oñ

@ñ-D©-V©-J@-©L SVP

We are in a hurry

Nous sommes pressés

N@ S©M PR©-S@

What do you recommend?

Qu'est-ce que vous recommandez?

K©S K@ V@ R@-K©-M@ñ-D@

Prease bring me...

Apportez-moi ... s'il vous plaît

@-POR-T@ MW@... SVP

Please bring us...

Apportez-nous...

@-POR-T@ N@...

I'm hungry

J'ai faim

ZH@ F@ñ

I'm thirsty

J'ai soif

ZH@ SW@F

Is service included?

le service est compris?

L@ S@R-V@S @ KOñ-PR@

The bill please

L'addition s'il vous plaît

L@-D@-S@-Oñ SVP

ORDERING BEVERAGES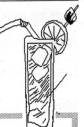

Ordering beverages is easy and a great way to practice your French! In many foreign countries you will have to request ice with your drinks.

Please bring me...

Apportez-moi ...

⬇ @-POR-T@ MW@...

coffee...	**tea...**
du café	du thé
D@ K@-F@	D@ T@

with cream

avec de la crème

@-V@K D@ L@ KR@M

with sugar

avec du sucre

@-V@K D@ S@-KR@

with lemon

avec du citron

@-V@K D@ S@-TR@ñ

with ice

avec de la glace

@-V@K D@ L@ GL@S

Soft drinks

Les sodas

LⒶ SⓄ-D(ah)

Milk

Le lait

L(uh) LⒶ

Hot chocolate

Le chocolat chaud

L(uh) SHⓄ-KⓄ-L(ah) SHⓄ

Juice

Le jus

L(uh) ZH(ew)

Orange juice

Le jus d'orange

L(uh) ZH(ew) DⓄ-R(ah)ñZH

Ice water

L'eau glacée

LⓄ GL(ah)-SⒶ

Mineral water

L'eau minérale

LⓄ M(EE)-NⒶ-R(ah)L

AT THE BAR

Bartender
Le bar man

L⒰ B⒜R M⒜N

The wine list please
La carte des vin

L⒜ K⒜RT D⒜ V⒜ñ SVP

Cocktail
le cocktail

L⒰ K⒜K-T⒜L

On the rocks
Aux glaçons

Ⓞ GL⒜-S⒪ñ

Straight
Sans glaçons

S⒜ñ GL⒜-S⒪ñ

With lemon
Àvec du citron

⒜-V⒠K D⒠W S⒠⒠-TR⒪ñ

PHRASEMAKER

I would like a glass of...

Je voudrais un verre...

ZH⏀ V⏀⏀-DR🅐 ⏀ñ V🅔R..

champagne

de champagne

D⏀ SH🅐ñ-P🅐ñ-Y⏀

beer

de bière

D⏀ B🅔🅔-🅔R

wine

de vin

D⏀ V🅐ñ

red wine

de vin rouge

D⏀ V🅐ñ R⏀⏀ZH

white wine

de vin blanc

D⏀ V🅐ñ BL🅐ñ

ORDERING BREAKFAST

In France breakfast, le petit déjeuner, is usually
small, consisting of a croissant or French bread
with butter and jam accompanied by café au lait,
hot tea or hot chocolate.

Bread

Le pain

L(uh) P(ã)ñ

Toast

Le toast

↓ L(uh) T(o)ST

---

with butter

avec du beurre

(ah)-V(ê)K D(ew) B(ou)R

---

with jam

avec de la confiture

(ah)-V(ê)K D(uh) L(ah) K(o)ñ-F(ee)-T(ew)R

Cereal

Le céréale

L(uh) S(A)-R(A)-(ah)L

PHRASEMAKER

I would like...

Je voudrais...

↓ZH⓪ V⓪-DR④...

two eggs...

deux oeufs...

D⓪ Z⓪...

with bacon

avec du bacon

④-VⓔK Dⓔ B④-K⓪ñ

with ham

avec du jambon

④-VⓔK Dⓔ ZH④M-B⓪ñ

with potatoes

avec des pommes de terre

④-VⓔK D④ P⓪M D⓪ TⓔR

HOW DO YOU WANT YOUR EGGS?

Scrambled

Brouillés

BR⓪-Y④

Fried

Sur le plat

SⓔR L⓪ PL④

LUNCH AND DINNER

Although you are encouraged to sample great French cuisine, it is important to be able to order foods you are familiar with. This section will provide words and phrases to help you.

I would like...

Je voudrais...

ZH⒰ V⒪⒪-DR⒜...

We would like...

Nous voudrions...

N⒪⒪ V⒪⒪-DR⒠⒠-O⒩...

Bring us...

Apportez-nous...

⒜-P⒪R-T⒜ N⒪⒪...

The lady would like...

La madame voudrait....

L⒜ M⒜-D⒜M V⒪⒪-DR⒜...

The gentleman would like...

Le monsieur voudrait...

L⒰ M⒰-SY⒪⒰ V⒪⒪-DR⒜...

STARTERS

Appetizers

Les hors d'oeuvres

LA OR-Dou-VRuh

Bread and butter

Le pain et le beurre

Luh Pañ A Luh Bour

Cheese

Le fromage

Luh FRO-MahZH

Fruit

Le fruit

Luh FRWEE

Salad

La salade

Lah Sah-LahD

Soup

La soupe

Lah SooP

MEATS

Beef
Le boeuf
L⒰ B⓪F

Beef Steak
Le bifteck
L⒰ B⒠F-T⒠K

Pork
Le porc
L⒰ P⓪RK

Ham
Le jambon
L⒰ ZH⒜M-B⓪ñ

Bacon
Le bacon
L⒰ B⒜-K⓪ñ

Lamb
L'agneau
L⒜-NY⓪

Veal
Le veau
L⒰ V⓪

POULTRY

Baked chicken

Le poulet au four

L⒰ P⒪⒪-L⒜ ⒪ F⒪⒪R

Broiled chicken

Le poulet grillé

L⒰ P⒪⒪-L⒜ GR⒠⒠-Y⒜

Fried chicken

Le poulet frit

L⒰ P⒪⒪-L⒜ FR⒠⒠

Duck

Le canard

L⒰ K⒜-N⒜R

Turkey

Le dinde

L⒰ D⒜ñD

Goose

L'oie

LW⒜

SEAFOOD

Fish
Le poisson
L(uh) PW(ah)-S(O)ñ

Lobster
L'homard
L(O)-M(ah)R

Oysters
Les huîtres
L(A) W(EE)-TR(uh)

Salmon
Le saumon
L(uh) S(O)-M(O)ñ

Shrimp
La crevette
L(ah) KR(ĕ)-V(ĕ)T

Trout
La truite
L(ah) TRW(EE)T

Tuna
Le thon
L(uh) T(O)ñ

OTHER ENTREES

Sandwich
Le sandwich

Hot dog
Le hot-dog
L⬤ H⬤T D⬤G

Hamburger
Le hamburger

French fries
Les frites
L⬤ FR⬤T

Pasta
Les pâtes
L⬤ P⬤T

Pizza
La pizza

VEGETABLES

Carrots

Les carottes

L@ K@h-R⊙T

Corn

Le maïs

L⓾ M@h-Œ

Mushrooms

Les champignons

L@ SH@hñ-PŒ-NY⊙ñ

Onions

Les oignons

L@ Z⊙-NY⊙ñ

Potato

La pomme de terre

L@h P⓾M D⓾ TêR

Rice

Le riz

L⓾ RŒ

Tomato

la tomate

L@h T⊙-M@hT

FRUITS

Apple

La pomme

L@h P@M

Banana

La banane

L@h B@h-N@h

Grapes

Les raisins

L@ R@-Z@ñ

Lemon

Le citron

L@h S@-TR@ñ

Orange

L'orange

L@-R@hñZH

Strawberry

La fraise

L@h FR@Z

Watermelon

La pastèque

L@h P@hS-T@K

DESSERT

Desserts
Les desserts

LⒶ DⒶ-SⓔR

Apple pie
La tarte aux pommes

Lⓐⓗ TⓐⓗRT Ⓞ PⓤⓗM

Cherry pie
La tarte aux cerises

Lⓐⓗ TⓐⓗRT Ⓞ Sⓔ-RⒺⒺS

Pastries
Les pâtisseries

LⒶ Pⓐⓗ-TⒺⒺ-Sⓔ-RⒺⒺ

Candy
Les bonbons

LⒶ BⓄñ BⓄñ

Ice cream
La glace

Lⓐⓗ GLⓐⓗS

Ice cream cone

La cone

L@h K@N

Chocolate

Au chocolat

@ SH@-K@-L@h

Strawberry

A la fraise

@h L@h FR@Z

Vanilla

A la vanille

@h L@h V@h-N@L

CONDIMENTS

Salt   **Pepper**

Le sel   Le poivre

Lᵘʰ SĕL   Lᵘʰ PWₐʰ-VRᵘʰ

Sugar

Le sucre

Lᵘʰ Sᵉʷ-KRᵘʰ

Mayonnaise

La mayonnaise

Lₐʰ Mₐ-YO-NĕZ

Butter

Le beurre

Lᵘʰ BᵒᵘR

Mustard

La moutarde

Lₐʰ Mᵒᵒ-TₐʰRD

Ketchup

Le ketchup

Lᵘʰ KĕT-CHᵘʰP

Vinegar and oil

La vinaigrette

Lₐʰ Vᵉᵉ-Nₐ-GRĕT

SETTINGS

A cup
Une tasse

A glass
Un verre

A spoon
Une cuillère

A fork
Une fourchette

A knife
Un couteau

A plate
Une assiette

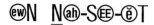

A napkin
Une serviette

@N S@R-V@E-@T

HOW DO YOU WANT IT COOKED?

Baked
Cuit au four

KW(EE)T Ⓞ F(oo)R

Broiled
Grillé

GR(EE)

Steamed
A l'étuvée

(ah) L(A)-T(ew)-V(A)

Fried
Frit

FRW(EE)

Rare
Saignant

S(A)-NY(ah)ñ

Medium
A point

(ah) PW(ah)ñ

Well done
Bien cuit

B(EE)-(a)ñ KW(EE)

PROBLEMS

I didn't order this

Je n'ai pas commandé ceci

ZH⒰ N⒜ P⒜ K⓪-M⒜N-D⒜ S⒰-S⒠

Is the bill correct?

Ill y a une erreur dans la note ?

⒠L ⒠ ⒜ ⒠wN ⒠R-R⒪⒰R
D⒜ñ L⒜ N⓪T

Bring me...

Apportez moi...

↓⒜-P⓪R-T⒜ MW⒜...

another spoon please

une autre cuillère s'il vous plaît

⒠wN N⓪-TR⒰ KW⒠-Y⒠R SVP

another fork please

une autre fourchette s'il vous plaît

⒠wN N⓪-TR⒰ F⒪⒪R-SH⒠T SVP

another plate please

une autre assiette s'il vous plaît

⒠wN N⓪-TR⒰ ⒜-S⒠-⒠T SVP

GETTING AROUND

Getting around in a foreign country can be an adventure in itself! Taxi and bus drivers do not always speak English, so it is essential to be able to give simple directions. The words and phrases in this chapter will help you get where you're going.

- Stationnement de Taxi indicates a taxi stand.

- Trains are used frequently by visitors to Europe. Schedules and timetables are easily understood. Arrive early to allow time for ticket purchasing and checking in and remember, trains leave on time!

- Le Métro or subway is an inexpensive underground train system in Paris. "M" signifies a metro stop!

- Check with your travel agent about special rail passes which allow unlimited travel within a set period of time.

SIGNS TO LOOK FOR:
BILLETS (TICKET OFFICE)
RENSEIGNEMENTS (INFORMATION)

KEY WORDS

Airport (See page 82)

L' aéroport

L@-A-R@-P@R

Bus Station / Bus Stop (See page 84)

Le gare routière
L'arrêt de bus

L@ G@R R@-T@-@R
L@-R@ D@ B@S

Car Rental Agency (See page 86)

L'agence de location

L@-ZH@ñS D@ L@-K@-S@-@ñ

Subway Station (See page 88)

Le métro

L@ M@-TR@

Taxi Stand (See page 90)

La station de taxis

L@ ST@-S@-@ñ D@ T@K-S@

Train Station (See page 88)

la gare

L@ G@R

AIR TRAVEL

Arrivals
Les arrivées

L__A__ Z__ah__-R__EE__-V__A__

Departures
Les départs

L__A__ D__A__-P__ah__R

Flight number...
Le vol numéro...

L__uh__ VOL N__ew__-M__A__-R__O__...

Airline
La ligne aérienne

L__ah__ L__EE__N-Y__uh__ __ah__-__A__-R__EE__-__ě__N

The gate
La porte

L__ah__ P__O__RT

Information
Les renseignements

L__A__ R__ah__ñ-S__ě__N-Y__uh__-M__ah__ñ

Ticket (airline)
Le billet

L__uh__ B__EE__-Y__A__

Reservations
Les réservations

L__A__ R__A__-S__ě__R-V__ah__-S__EE__-O__ñ

Note: See arrival section for phrases on baggage

I would like a seat...

Je voudrais une place...

ZH⓪ V⊙⊙-DR④ ⓔⓌN PL④S...

in the no smoking section

dans la zone non fumeurs

D④ñ L④ Z⊙N N⊙ñ F⊕Ⓦ-M⊙⊙R

next to the window

à coté de la fenêtre

④ K⊙-T④ D⓪ L④

F⓪-Nĕ-TR⓪

on the aisle

au couloir

⊙ K⊙⊙L-W④R

near the exit

près de la sortie

PR④ D⓪ L④ S⊙R-T€€

in first class

à première classe

④ PR⓪M-YĕR KL④S

THE BUS

Bus

L'autobus

LO-TO-Bew S

Where is the bus stop?

Où est l'arrêt d'autobus?

oo A Lah-Ré DO-TO-BewS

Do you go to...?

Vous allez à...?

Voo Zah-LA ah...

What is the fare?

C'est combien?

SA KOñ-BEE-añ

Do I need exact change?

Est-ce que j'ai besoin de monnaie précise?

éS-Kuh ZHA Buh-ZWañ Duh
MO-NA PRA-SEES

How often do the buses run?

Les autobus sont tous les combien?

LA ZO-TO-BewS SOñ Too LA
KOñ-BEE-añ

PHRASEMAKER

Please tell me...

Dites-moi....

↓ DEET MWah...

---

which bus goes to...

quel autobus va à...

Kẽ LO-TO-Bews Vah ah...

---

what time the bus leaves

à quelle heure est-ce que l'autobus départ

ah Kẽ LouR ẽS-Kuh
LO-TO-Bews DA-PahR

---

where the bus stop is

où est l'arrêt d'autobus

oo A Lah-Rẽ DO-TO-Bews

---

where to get off

où est-ce qu'il faut descendre

oo ẽS-KEEL FO DA-Sahñ-DRuh

BY CAR

Fill it up

Faites le plein

F**ẽ**T L**uh** PL**ã**ñ

Please check...

Vérifiez...

↓ V**Ⓐ**-R**Ⓔ**-FY**Ⓐ**...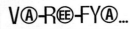

the oil

l'huile

L**ⓔⱳ**-**Ⓔ**L

the battery

la batterie

L**ah** B**ah**-T**ẽ**-R**Ⓔ**

the tires

les pneus

L**Ⓐ** P**uh**-N**ⓞⱳ**

the water

l'eau

L**Ⓞ**

the brakes

les freins

L**Ⓐ** FR**ẽ**N

Can you help me?

Vous pouvez m'aider?

V⃝ P⃝-V⃝ M⃝-D⃝

My car won't start

Ma voiture ne démarre pas

M⃝ VW⃝-T⃝R N⃝
D⃝-M⃝R P⃝

I need a mechanic

J'ai besoin d'un garagiste

ZH⃝ B⃝-ZW⃝ñ D⃝ñ
G⃝-R⃝-ZH⃝ST

Can you fix it?

Vous pouvez la réparer?

V⃝ P⃝-V⃝ L⃝ R⃝-P⃝-R⃝

What will it cost?

Combien est-ce que cela coûte?

K⃝ñ-B⃝-⃝ñ ⃝S-K⃝ S⃝-L⃝ K⃝T

How long will it take?

Ça va prendre combien de temps?

S⃝ V⃝ PR⃝ñ-DR⃝
K⃝ñ-B⃝-⃝ñ D⃝ T⃝ñ

SUBWAYS AND TRAINS

Where is the subway station?

Où est le métro?

(oo) (A) L(uh) M(A)-TR(O)

Where is the train station?

Où est la gare?

(oo) (A) L(ah) G(ah)R

A one way ticket please

Un aller s'il vous plaît

(uh)ñ N(ah)-L(A) SVP

A round trip ticket

Un aller et retour

(uh)ñ N(ah)-L(A) (A) R(uh)-T(oo)R

First class

Première classe

PR(uh)M-Y(ë)R KL(ah)S

Second class

Deuxième classe

D(ou)-Z(EE)-(ë)M   KL(ah)S

Which train do I take to go to...?

Quel train est-ce que je prends pour aller à...?

KĔL TRȃñ ĕS-Kᵘʰ ZHᵘʰ
PRȃñ PᵒᵒR ᵃʰ-LⒶ ᵃʰ...

What is the fare?

C'est combien?

SⒶ KⓄñ-BⒺⒺ-ȃñ

Is this seat taken?

La place est libre?

Lᵃʰ PLᵃʰS Ⓐ LⒺⒺ-BRᵘʰ

Do I have to change trains?

Est-ce qu'il faut changer de train?

ĕS-KⒺⒺL FⓄ SHᵃʰñ-ZHⒶ
Dᵘʰ TRȃñ

Does this train stop at...

Est-ce que ce train s'arrête à...

ĕS-Kᵘʰ Sᵘʰ TRȃñ
Sᵃʰ-RⒺ Tᵃʰ...

Where are we?

Où sommes-nous?

ᵒᵒ SⓄM Nᵒᵒ

TAXI

Can you call a taxi for me?

Appelez-moi un taxi s'il vous plaît?

ⓐ-PLⒶ MWⓐ ⓤñ Tⓐ-K-SⒺ SVP

Are you available?

Vous êtes libre?

Vⓞⓞ Z̲ě̃T LⒺ-BRⓤ

I want to go...

Je voudrais aller...

ZHⓤ Vⓞⓞ-DRⒶ Z̲ⓐ-LⒶ...

Stop here please

Arrêtez ici s'il vous plaît

ⓐ-Rě-TⒶ Z̲Ⓔ-SⒺ SVP

Please wait

Attendez s'il vous plaît

ⓐ-Tⓐñ-DⒶ SVP

How much do I owe?

Combien est-ce que je dois?

KⓄñ-BⒺ-ⓐ̃ñ ěS-Kⓤ

ZHⓤ DWⓐ

PHRASEMAKER

I would like to go...

Je voudrais aller...

ZH⒰ V⓪⓪-DR⒜ Z⒜-L⒜...

to the hotel...

à l'hôtel...

⒜ L⓪-T⒠L...

to this address

à cet adresse

⒜ S⒠T ⒜-DR⒠S

to the airport

à l'aéroport

⒜ L⒜-⒜-R⓪-P⓪R

to the subway station

au métro

⓪ M⒜-TR⓪

to the hospital

à l'hôpital

⒜ L⓪-P⒠⒠-T⒜L

to the bank

à la banque

⒜ L⒜ B⒜NK

SHOPPING

Whether you plan a major shopping spree or just need to purchase some basic necessities,  the following information is useful.

- **Palais de Congrès de Paris** and **Forum des Halles** are popular shopping centers in Paris.

- Department stores are open Monday through Saturday between 9:30 a.m. and 6 p.m. Smaller stores may close for lunch between noon and 2 p.m.

- Always keep receipts for everything you buy!

SIGNS TO LOOK FOR:

BOULANGERIE (BAKERY)
BUREAU DE TABAC (SMOKE SHOP-STAMPS)
CARTES POSTALES (POST CARDS)
CONFECTION DAMES (WOMEN'S CLOTHES)
CONFECTION HOMMES (MEN'S CLOTHES)
GRAND MAGASIN   (DEPARTMENT STORE)
LIBRAIRIE (BOOK STORE)
CHAUSSURES (SHOES)
SUPERMARCHE (SUPERMARKET)

KEY WORDS

Credit card

La carte de crédit

L@ K@RT D@ KR@-D©

Money

L'argent

L@R-ZH@ñ

Receipt

Le reçu

L@ R@-S©

Sale

La vente

L@ V@ñT

Store

Le magasin

L@ M@-G@-Z@ñ

Traveler's checks

Les chèques de voyage

L@ SH@K D@ VW@-Y@ZH

USEFUL PHRASES

Do you sell...?

Est-ce que vous vendez...?

ĕS-K(uh) V(oo) V(ah)ñ-D(A)...

Do you have...?

Avez-vous...?

(ah)-V(A) V(oo)...

I want to buy...

Je voudrais acheter...

ZH(uh) V(oo)-DR(A) (ah)SH-T(A)...

How much?

Combien?

K(O)ñ-B(EE)-(a)ñ

When are the shops open?

Quand est-ce que les boutiques s'ouvrent?

K(ah)ñ T̲ĕS-K(uh) L(A)
B(oo)-T(EE)K S(oo)-VR(uh)

No thank you

Non, merci

N(O)ñ M(ĕ)R-S(EE)

I´m just looking

Je regarde seulement

ZH(uh) R(uh)-G(ah)RD S(ou)L-M(ah)ñ

It's very expensive

C'est trop cher

S(A) TR(O) SH(ê)R

Can't you give me a discount?

Pouvez -vous me donner un prix réduit?

P(oo)-V(A) V(oo) M(uh) D(O)-N(A) (uh)ñ

PR(EE) R(A)-DW(EE)

I'll take it!

Je le prendrai!

ZH(uh) L(uh) PR(ah)ñ-DR(A)

I'd like a receipt please

Je voudrais un reçu

ZH(uh) V(oo)-DR(A) (uh)ñ R(uh)-S(ew)

I want to return this

Je voudrais rendre ceci

ZH(uh) V(oo)-DR(A) R(ah)ñ-DR(uh) S(uh)-S(EE)

It doesn't fit

Ça ne va pas

S(ah) N(uh) V(ah) P(ah)

PHRASEMAKER

I'm looking for...

Je cherche...

↓ ZH(uh) SH(ê)RSH...

---

a bakery

une boulangerie

(ew)N B(oo)-L(ah)ñ-ZH(uh)-R(ee)

---

a bank

une banque

(ew)N B(ah)NK

---

a barber shop

un coiffeur

(uh)ñ KW(ah)-F(ou)R

---

a book store

une librairie

(ew)N L(ee)-BR(ê)-R(ee)

---

a camera shop

un photo station

(uh)ñ F(o)-T(o) ST(ah)-S(ee)-(o)ñ

↓

a florist shop

un fleuriste

ⓤhñ FLⓞⓤ-RⓔⓔST

a hair salon

une coiffure

ⓔwN KWⓐh-FⓔwR

a pharmacy

une pharmacie

ⓔwN FⓐhR-Mⓐh-Sⓔⓔ

Do you sell...

Est-ce que vous vendez...

↓ ⓔS-Kⓤh Vⓞⓞ Vⓐhñ-Dⓐ...

aspirin?

l'aspirine?

LⓐhS-Pⓔⓔ-RⓔⓔN

cigarettes?

les cigarettes?

Lⓐ Sⓔⓔ-Gⓐh-Rⓔ̃T

dresses?   shirts?

les robes?   les chemises?

Lⓐ RⓞB   Lⓐ SHⓤh-MⓔⓔZ

↓

deodorant?

le déodorant?

L@h D@-@-D@-R@hñ

film?

la pellicule?

L@h P@-L@-K@wL

pantyhose?

le collant?

L@h K@-L@hñ

perfume?

le parfum?

L@h P@hR-F@hñ

razor blades?

les lames de rasoir?

L@ L@hM D@h R@h-SW@hR

shaving cream?

la crème à raser?

L@h KR@M @h R@h-S@

soap?

le savon?

L@h S@h-V@ñ

shampoo?

le shampooing?

L@h SH@hM-P@-@N

sunglasses?

les lunettes de soleil?

L(A) L(ew)-N(e)T D(uh) S(O)-L(A)

sunscreen?

la crème solaire?

L(ah) KR(e)M S(O)-L(e)R

toothbrushes?

les brosses à dents?

L(A) BR(O) S(ah) D(ah)ñ

toothpaste?

le dentifrice?

L(uh) D(ah)ñ-T(EE)-FR(EE)S

water? (bottled)

l'eau nature?

L(O) N(ah)-T(ew)R

water? (mineral)

L'eau minérale?

L(O) M(EE)-N(A)-R(ah)L

ESSENTIAL SERVICES

Placing phone calls, mailing postcards and exchanging money are a few tasks you may need to perform while traveling.

THE BANK

As a traveler in a foreign country your primary contact with banks will be to exchange money.

- Have your passport handy when changing money.

- Change enough funds before leaving home to pay for tips, food and transportation to your final destination.

- Generally, you will receive a better rate of exchange at a bank than at an exchange office or airport.

- Current exchange rates are posted in banks and published daily in city newspapers.

SIGNS TO LOOK FOR:

BANQUE (BANK)
BUREAU DE CREDIT (BANK)
BUREAU DE CHANGE (EXCHANGE OFFICE)

KEY WORDS

Bank
La banque

Lah Bahnk

Exchange office
Le bureau de change

Luh Bew-Ro Duh SHahñZH

Money
L'argent

LahR-ZHahñ

Money order
Le mandat-poste

Luh Mahñ-Dah Post

Travelers checks
Les chèques de voyage

La SHëK Duh VWah-Yahzh

Currencies
Le franc

Luh FRahñ

Le centime

Luh Sahñ-TëEM

USEFUL PHRASES

Where is the bank?

Où est la banque?

ⓞⓞ   Ⓐ   Lⓐⓗ   BⓐⓗNK

What time does the bank open?

A quelle heure est-ce que la banque s'ouvre?

ⓐⓗ   Kⓔ̆   LⓞⓤR   ⓔ̆S-Kⓤⓗ   Lⓐⓗ
BⓐⓗNK   Sⓞⓞ-VRⓤⓗ

Where is the Exchange Office?

Où est le bureau de change?

ⓞⓞ   Ⓐ   Lⓤⓗ   Bⓔⓦ-Rⓞ   Dⓤⓗ   SHⓐⓗñZH

What time does the Exchange Office open?

A quelle heure s'ouvre le bureau de change?

ⓐⓗ   Kⓔ̆   LⓞⓤR   Sⓞⓞ-VRⓤⓗ
Lⓤⓗ   Bⓔⓦ-Rⓞ   Dⓤⓗ   SHⓐⓗñZH

Can I change dollars here?

Puis-je changer des dollars ici?

PWⓔⓔ-ZHⓤⓗ   SHⓐⓗñ-ZHⒶ   DⒶ
Dⓞ-LⓐⓗR   ⓔⓔ-Sⓔⓔ

Can you change this?

Pouvez-vous changer ceci?

POO-VA VOO SHahñ-ZHA Suh-SEE

What is the exchange rate?

Quel est le taux de change?

KE LA Luh TO Duh SHahñZH

I would like large bills

Je voudrais de grands billets

ZHuh VOO-DRA Duh
GRahñ BEE-YA

I would like small bills

Je voudrais de petits billets

ZHuh VOO-DRA Duh
Puh-TEE BEE-YA

I need change

J'ai besoin de monnaie

ZHA Buh-ZWAñ Duh MO-NA

Do you have an ATM

Avez vous un GAB?

ah-VA VOO uhñ ZHA ah BA

POST OFFICE

If you are planning on sending letters and postcards, be sure to send them early so that you don't arrive home before they do. **PTT** or **POSTE** identifies the post office.

KEY WORDS

Air mail

Par avion

P@R @h-V㎍-O̅n̅

Letter

La lettre

L@ L@-TR@

Post office

La poste

L@ P@ST

Postcard

La carte postale

L@ K@RT P@S-T@L

Stamp

Le timbre

L@ T@n̅-BR@

USEFUL PHRASES

Where is the post office?

Où est la poste?

ⓞⓞ Ⓐ Lⓐⓗ PⓞST

What time does the post office open?

A quelle heure est-ce que la poste s'ouvre?

ⓐⓗ Kⓔ LⓞⓤR ⓔS-Kⓤⓗ Lⓐⓗ PⓞST Sⓞⓞ-VRⓤⓗ

I need...

J'ai besoin...

↓ ZHⒶ Bⓤⓗ-ZWⓐñ...

stamps

de timbres

Dⓤⓗ Tⓐñ-BRⓤⓗ

an envelope

d'une enveloppe

DⓔⓦN ⓐñ-Vⓔ-LⓞP

a pen

d'un stylo

Dⓤⓗñ STⓔⓔ-Lⓞ

TELEPHONE

Placing phone calls in a foreign country can be a test of will and stamina! Besides the obvious language barriers, service can vary greatly from one town to the next.

- If you have a choice do not call from your hotel room. Service charges can add a hefty amount to your bill.

- In France, phone calls can be made from the post office.

- To dial direct to the U.S. from a new public pay phone dial: 19 + 1 + area code + number.

SIGNS TO LOOK FOR:

CABINE TELEPHONIQUE (TELEPHONE BOOTH)
TELEPHONE (TELEPHONE)
PTT (POST-TELEPHONE-TELEGRAPH)

KEY WORDS

Information

Les renseignements

LⒶ RⒶñ-SĕN-Yⓢ-MⒶñ

Long distance

De communication interurbaine

Dⓢ KⓈ-MⒼ-NⒼ-KⒶ-SⒼ-Oñ

ãñ-Tⓢ-ⒼR-BĕN

Operator

Le standardiste

Lⓢ STⒶN-DⒶR-DⒼST

Phone book

L'annuaire

LⒶ-NⒼ-ĕR

Public telephone

Le téléphone public

Lⓢ TⒶ-LⒶ-FⓈN PⒼ-BLⒼK

Telephone

Le téléphone

Lⓢ TⒶ-LⒶ-FⓈN

USEFUL PHRASES

May I use your telephone?

Puis-je me servir de votre téléphone?

PWEE-ZHuh Muh SĕR-VEER   Duh
VO-TRuh TA-LA-FON

Operator, I don't speak French

Madame (monsieur) le standardiste,
je ne parle pas français

MAh-DAhM Luh STAhN-DAhR-DEEST
ZHuhN-uh PAhRL PAh FRAhñ-SA

I want to call...

Je voudrais téléphoner ...

↓ ZHuh VOO-DRA...

1 un uhñ	**2** deux Dou
3 trois TRWAh	**4** quatre KAh-TRuh
5 cinq SANK	**6** six SEES
7 sept SĕT	**8** huit WEET
9 neuf NouF	**0** zéro ZA-RO

PHRASEMAKER

I would like to make a call...

Je voudrais donner un coup de téléphone...

ZH⒰ V⊚-DR⒜ D⊙-N⒜

↓ ⒰ñ K⊚ D⒰ T⒜-L⒜-FON...

long distance

de communication interurbaine

D⒰ K⊙-M⒠-N⒠-K⒜-S⒠-⊙ñ

⒜ñ-T⒰-⒠R-B⒠N

collect

de communication en P.C.V.

D⒰ K⊙-M⒠-N⒠-K⒜-S⒠-⊙ñ

⒜ñ P⒜ S⒜ V⒜

person to person

de communication avec préavis

D⒰ K⊙-M⒠-N⒠-K⒜-S⒠-⊙ñ

⒜-V⒠K PR⒜-⒜-V⒠

to the United States

aux Etats-Unis

⊙ Z⒜-T⒜-Z⒠-N⒠

SIGHTSEEING AND ENTERTAINMENT

In most towns in France you will find tourist information offices. Here you can usually obtain brochures, maps, historical information, bus and train schedules.

THINGS TO SEE IN PARIS

L'Arc de Triomphe
L@RK D@h TR@@-O@F

L'opéra
L@-P@-R@h

Les Champs-Elysées
L@ SH@h-Z@-L@@-S@

Le Tour Eiffel
L@h T@R @@-F@L

Notre Dame
N@-TR@h D@M

Le Louvre
L@h L@-VR@h

KEY WORDS

Admission
L'entrée

Lⓐñ-TRⓐ

Map
Le plan

Lⓤh PLⓐñ

Reservation
La réservation

Lⓐ Rⓐ-Sⓔ̃R-Vⓐh-SⒺⒺ-Ⓞñ

Ticket
Le ticket

Lⓤh TⒺⒺ-Kⓐ

Tour
La visite

Lⓐ VⒺⒺ-ZⒺⒺT

Tour guide
Le guide

Lⓤh GⒺⒺD

USEFUL PHRASES

Where is the tourist office?

Où est le syndicat d'Initiative?

(oo) (A) L(uh) S(EE)N-D(EE)-K(ah)

D(EE)-N(EE)-S(EE)-(ah)-T(EE)V

Is there a tour to...?

Y a-t-il une visite guidée à...?

(EE) (ah)-T(EE)L (ew)N

V(EE)-Z(EE)T G(EE)-D(A) (ah)...

Where do I buy a ticket?

Où puis-je acheter un ticket?

(oo) PW(EE)-ZH(uh) (ah)SH-T(A)

(uh)ñ T(EE)-K(A)

How much does the tour cost?

Combien coûte la visite?

K(O)ñ-B(EE)-(ã)ñ K(oo)T L(ah) V(EE)-Z(EE)T

How long does the tour take?

La visite prend combien de temps?

L(ah) V(EE)-Z(EE)T PR(ah)ñ

K(O)ñ-B(EE)-(ã)ñ D(uh) T(ah)ñ

Does the guide speak English?

Est-ce que le guide parle anglais?

ⓔS-Kⓤh Lⓤh GⓔⒺD Pⓐ︎RL ⓐ︎ñ-GLⒶ

Are children free?

Y a-t-il un tarif pour enfants?

ⒺⒺ ⓐ︎-TⒺⒺL ⓤhñ Tⓐ︎-RⒺⒺF Pⓞ︎R
ⓐ︎ñ-Fⓐ︎ñ

What time does the show start?

A quelle heure commence le spectacle?

ⓐ︎ Kⓔ̃ Lⓞ︎uR Kⓞ-Mⓐ︎ñS Lⓤh
SPⓔ̃K-Tⓐ︎-KLⓤh

Do I need reservations?

Il faut avoir des réservations?

ⒺⒺL Fⓞ ⓐ︎-VWⓐ︎R DⒶ
RⒶ-Sⓔ̃R-Vⓐ︎-SⒺⒺ-Ⓞñ

Where can we go dancing?

Où est-ce qu'on peut danser?

ⓞ︎ⓞ ⓔ̃S KⓞñR Pⓞ︎u Dⓐ︎ñ-SⒶ

Is there a minimum cover charge?

Y a-t-il un prix d'entrée?

ⒺⒺ ⓐ︎-TⒺⒺL ⓤhñ PRⒺⒺ Dⓐ︎ñ-TRⒶ

PHRASEMAKER

May I invite you...

Je vous invite...

ZH⒰ V⒰ Z⒜ñ-V⒠T...

to a concert?

à un concert?

⒜ⓗ ⒰ⓗñ K⒪ñ-S⒠R

to dance?

à danser?

⒜ⓗ D⒜ⓗñ-S⒜

to dinner?

au dîner?

⒪ D⒠-N⒜

to the movies?

au cinéma?

⒪ S⒠-N⒜-M⒜ⓗ

to the theater?

au théâtre?

⒪ T⒜-⒜ⓗ-TR⒰

Where can I find...

Où se trouve...

↓ ⓞⓞ Sⓤⓗ TRⓞⓞV...

a golf course?

un terrain de golf?

ⓤⓗñ Tⓔ̆-Rⓐ̃ñ Dⓤⓗ GⓄLF

a health club?

un centre sportif?

ⓤⓗñ Sⓐⓗñ-TRⓤⓗ SPⓄR-Tⓔ̆F

a swimming pool?

une piscine?

ⓔ̆wN Pⓔ̆Ⓔ-Sⓔ̆ⓔN

a tennis court?

un terrain de tennis?

ⓤⓗñ Tⓔ̆-Rⓐ̃ñ Dⓤⓗ Tⓔ̆-Nⓔ̆ⓔS

HEALTH

Hopefully you will not need medical attention on your trip. If you do, it is important to communicate basic information regarding your condition.

- Check with your insurance company before leaving home to find out if you are covered in a foreign country.

- Have your prescriptions translated before you leave home.

- Take a small first aid kit with you. Include Band Aids, aspirin, cough syrup, throat lozenges, and vitamins.

- Your Embassy or Consulate should be able to assist you in finding health care.

- A GREEN CROSS indicates Pharmacy, where minor treatment can be handled by the pharmacist.

SIGNS TO LOOK FOR:

Ⓗ (HOSPITAL)

GREEN CROSS (PHARMACY)

KEY WORDS

Ambulance
L'ambulance

L@ñ-B@-L@ñS

Dentist
Le dentiste

L@ D@ñ-T@ST

Doctor
Le médecin

L@ M@-D@-S@ñ

Emergency!
L'urgence!

L@R-ZH@ñS

Hospital
L'hôpital

L@-P@-T@L

Prescription
La prescription

L@ PR@-SKR@P-S@-@ñ

USEFUL PHRASES

I am sick

Je suis malade

ZH⒰ SW㊸ M㋐-L㋐D

I need a doctor

J'ai besoin d'un docteur

ZH㋐ B⒰-ZW㋐ñ D⒰ñ D㋐K-T⒪R

It's an emergency!

C'est une urgence!

S㋐ T㋔ N⒪R-ZH㋐ñS

Where is the nearest hospital?

Oú est l'hôpital le plus proche?

⒪⒪ Ⓐ L⒪-P㋸-T㋐L L⒰ PL㋔

PR⒪SH

Call an ambulance!

Faites venir une ambulance!

F㋒T V⒰-N㋸R

㋔ N㋐ñ-B㋔-L㋐ñS

I'm allergic to...

Je suis allergique à...

ZH(uh) SW(EE) Z(ah)-L(ẽ)R-ZH(EE) K(ah)...

I'm pregnant

Je suis enceinte

ZH(uh) SW(EE) Z(ah)ñ-S(ã)ñT

I'm diabetic

Je suis diabétique

ZH(uh) SW(EE) D(EE)-(ah)-B(A)-T(EE)K

I have a heart condition

Je suis cardiaque

ZH(uh) SW(EE) K(ah)R-D(EE)-(ah)-K(uh)

I have high blood pressure

Je fais de l'hypertension

ZH(uh) F(A) D(uh)

L(EE)-P(ẽ)R-T(ah)ñ-S(EE)-O(ñ)

I have low blood pressure

Je fais de l'hypotension

ZH(uh) F(A) D(uh)

L(EE)-P(O)-T(ah)ñ-S(EE)-O(ñ)

PHRASEMAKER

I need...

J'ai besoin...

↓ ZH④ B⑩-ZW④ñ...

---

a doctor

d'un docteur

D⑩ñ D⑧K-T⑩R

---

a dentist

d'un dentiste

D⑩ñ D⑧ñ-T㊉ST

---

a nurse

d'une infirmière

D㋐ N̲④ñ-F㋐R-M㋐-ě̆R

---

an optician

d'un opticien

D⑩ñ N̲⑩P-T㋐-S㋐-④ñ

---

a pharmacist

d'un pharmacien

D⑩ñ F⑧R-M⑧-S㋐-④ñ

(AT THE PHARMACY)

Do you have...?

Avez-vous...?

⬇ @h-V@ V@...

aspirin?

l'aspirine?

L@S-P@-R@N

band aids?

des bandages?

D@ B@ñ-D@ZH

cough medicine?

le sirop contre la toux?

L@ S@-R@ K@ñ-TR@

L@ T@

ear drops?

les gouttes pour les oreilles?

L@ G@T P@R L@ Z@-R@-Y@

eye drops?

les gouttes pour les yeux?

L@ G@T P@R L@ Z@-Y@

PHRASES FOR BUSINESS TRAVELERS

It is important to show appreciation and interest in another person's language and culture, particularly when doing business. A few well pronounced phrases can make a great impression.

KEY WORDS

Appointment

Le rendez-vous

L(uh) R(ah)ñ-D(A)-V(oo)

Meeting

La réunion

L(ah) R(A)-(ew)N-Y(O)ñ

Marketing

Le marketing

L(uh) M(ah)R-K(ē)-T(EE)N

Presentation

La présentation

L(ah) PR(A)-S(ē)N-T(ah)-S(EE)-(O)ñ

Sales

Les ventes

L(A) V(ah)ñT

USEFUL PHRASES

I have an appointment

J'ai rendez-vous

ZH Ⓐ   RⒶⓃ-DⒶ-VⓄⓄ

I want to make an appointment with...

Je voudrais faire rendez-vous avec...

ZHⓊ   VⓄⓄ-DRⒶ   FⒺR

RⒶⓃ-DⒶ-VⓄⓄ   Ⓐⓗ-VⒺK...

Here is my card

Voici ma carte

VWⒶⓗ-SⒺⒺ   MⒶⓗ   KⒶⓗRT

Can we get an interpreter?

J'ai besoin d'un interprète?

ZHⒶ   BⓊⓗ-ZWⒶⓃ   DⓊⓗⓃ

NⒶⓃ-TⒺR-PRⒺT

May I speak to Mr...?

Puis-je parler à Monsieur...?

PWⒺⒺ-ZHⓊⓗ   PⒶⓗR-LⒶ   Ⓐⓗ   MⓊⓗ-SYⓄⓤ...

May I speak to Mrs...?

Puis-je parler à Madame...?

PWⒺⒺ-ZHⓊⓗ   PⒶⓗR-LⒶ   Ⓐⓗ   MⒶⓗ-DⒶⓗM...

PHRASEMAKER

I need...

J'ai besoin...

↓ ZH︎Ⓐ B⑩-ZWⓐñ...

---

a computer

d'un ordinateur

D⑩ñ N︎Ⓞ︎R-D︎Ⓔ︎Ⓔ-N︎ah-T⑩R

---

a copy machine

d'un copieur

D⑩ñ K︎Ⓞ-P︎Ⓔ︎Ⓔ-⑩R

---

a conference room

d'une salle de conférences

D︎Ⓔ︎wN S︎ahL D⑩ K︎Ⓞñ-F︎Ⓐ-R︎ahñS

---

a fax machine

d'un télécopieur

D⑩ñ T︎Ⓐ-L︎Ⓐ-K︎Ⓞ-P︎Ⓔ︎Ⓔ-⑩R

---

an interpreter

d'un interprète

D⑩ñ N︎Ⓐñ-T︎Ⓔ︎R-PR︎Ⓔ︎T

↓

a lawyer

d'un avocat

Dⓤⓗñ Nⓐⓗ-VⓄ-Kⓐⓗ

a notary

d'un notaire

Dⓤⓗñ NⓄ-Tⓔ̆R

overnight delivery

de livraison exprès

Dⓤⓗ LⒺⒺ-VRⓐ-SⓄñ ⓔ̆KS-PRⓔ̆

paper

de papier

Dⓤⓗ Pⓐⓗ-PⒺⒺ-ⓐ

a pen

d'un stylo

Dⓤⓗñ STⒺⒺ-LⓄ

a pencil

d'un crayon

Dⓤⓗñ KRⓐ-Ⓞñ

a secretary

d'un secrétaire

Dⓤⓗñ Sⓔ̆-KRⓔ̆-Tⓔ̆R

GENERAL INFORMATION

THE DAYS

Monday
lundi
Luñ-DEE

Tuesday
mardi
Mah R-DEE

Wednesday
mercredi
Mĕ R-KRuh-DEE

Thursday
jeudi
ZHou-DEE

Friday
vendredi
Vahñ-DRuh-DEE

Saturday
samedi
Sah M-DEE

Sunday
dimanche
DEE-MahñSH

THE MONTHS

January
janvier
ZHahñ-VEE-A

February
février
FA-VREE-A

March
mars
Mah RS

April
avril
ah V-REEL

May
mai
MA

June
juin
ZHOO-âñ

July
juillet
ZHWEE-A

August
août
OOT

September
septembre
SëP-Tahñ-BRuh

October
octobre
OK-TO-BRuh

November
novembre
NO-Vahñ-BRuh

December
décembre
DA-Sahñ-BRuh

Spring
le printemps
Luh PRâñ-Tahñ

Summer
l'été
LA-TA

Autumn
l'automne
LO-TOM

Winter
l'hiver
LEE-VëR

NUMBERS

0	1	2
zéro	Un	Deux
ZA-RO	uhñ	Dou

3	4	5
Trois	Quatre	Cinq
TRWah	Kah-TRuh	SãNK

6	7	8
Six	Sept	Huit
SEES	SéT	WEET

9	10	11
Neuf	Dix	Onze
NouF	DEES	OñZ

12	13	14
Douze	Treize	Quatorze
DooZ	TRéZ	Kah-TORZ

15	16	17
Quinze	Seize	Dix-sept
KãñZ	SéZ	DEE-SéT

18	19
Dix-huit	Dix-neuf
DEEZ-WEET	DEEZ-NouF

20	**30**
Vingt	Trente
Vãñ	TR@ñT

40	**50**
Quarante	Cinquante
Kẽ-R@ñT	Sãñ-K@ñT

100	**1000**
Cent	Mille
S@ñ	MEEL

1,000,000

Millon

MEE-LEE-Oñ

COLORS

Black

Noir (m) Noire (f)

NW@hR

Blue

Bleu (m) Bleue (f)

BLou

Brown

Brun (m)   Brune (f)

BRuhñ   BRewN

Gold

Or

OR

Gray

Gris (m)   Grise (f)

GREE   GREES

Green

Vert (m)   Verte (m)

VeR   VeRT

Orange

Orange

O-RahñZH

Pink

Rose

ROZ

Purple

Violet (m)   Violette (f)

VEE-O-LA   VEE-O-LёT

Red

Rouge

ROOZH

White

Blanc (m)   Blanche (f)

BLahñ   BLahñSH

Yellow

Jaune

ZHON

DICTIONARY

Gender of nouns and adjectives is indicated by an **(m)** for masculine and an **(f)** for feminine, where appropriate.

Each English entry is followed by the French spelling and the EPLS spelling.

A

a, an un/ñ une (f) ewN

a lot beaucoup BO-Koo

able (to be) pouvoir Poo-VW@R

above au dessus (de) O D/uh-Sew D/uh

accident l'accident (m) L@K-SEE-D@hñ

accommodation le logement L/uh LOZH-M@hñ

account le compte L/uh KOñT

address l'adresse (f) L@h-DRES

admission l'entrée (f) L@hñ-TR@

afraid (to be) avoir peur @h-VW@R P/ooR

after après @h-PR@

afternoon l'après-midi (m) L@h-PR@ MEE-DEE

agency l'agence (m) L@h-ZH@hñS

air conditioning d'air climatisé (m) D@R KLEE-M@h-TEES

aircraft l'avion (m) L@h-VEE-Oñ

airline la ligne aérienne L@h L@N @h-@-REE-@N

airport l'aéroport (m) L@h-@-RO-POR

aisle couloir KooL-W@R

all tout (m) Too toute (f) TooT

almost presque PR@S-K/uh

alone seul S/oolL

also aussi O-S@

always toujours Too-ZHooR

ambulance l'ambulance (f) L@hñ-Bew-L@hñS

American américain (m) ah-MA-REE-Kañ
 américaine (f) ah-MA-REE-KEN
and et A
another un autre uñ NO-TRuh
anything quelque chose KEL-Kuh SHOZ
apartment l'appartement (m) Lah-PahR-Tuh-Mañ
appetizers les hors-d'oeuvres (m) LA OR-Dou-VRuh
apple la pomme Lah PuhM
appointment le rendez-vous Luh Rañ-DA-Voo
April avril ah-VREEL
arrival l'arrivée (f) Lah-REE-VA
arrive (to) arriver ah-REE-VA
ashtray le cendrier Luh Sañ-DREE-A
aspirin l'aspirine (f) Lah-SPEE-REN
attention l'attention (f) Lah-Tañ-SEE-Oñ
August aout ooT
author l'auteur (m) LO-Tour
automobile l'automobile (f) LO-TO-MO-BEEL
autumn l'automme LO-TOñ
avenue l'avenue Lah-Vuh-New
awful affreux (m) ah-FRou affreuse (f) ah-FRouZ
B
baby le bébé Luh BA-BA
babysitter le garde-bébé Luh GahRD BA-BA
bacon le bacon Luh Bah-KOñ
bad mauvais (m) MO-VA mauvaise (f) MO-VEZ
bag le sac Luh SahK
baggage les bagages (m) LA Bah-GahZH
baked au four O FooR
bakery la boulangerie Lah Boo-Lañ-ZHuh-REE
banana la banane Lah Bah-NahN

bandage le bandage L(uh)   B(ah)N-D(ah)ZH
bank la banque L(ah)   B(ah)ñK
barber shop le coiffeur L(uh)   KW(ah)-F(ou)R
bartender le barman L(uh)   B(ah)R M(ah)N
bath la bain L(ah)   B(ah)ñ
bathing suit le maillot de bains L(uh)   M(ah)-Y(O)   D(uh)   B(ah)ñ
bathroom la salle de bains L(ah)   S(ah)L   D(uh)   B(ah)ñ
battery la batterie L(uh)   B(ah)-T(uh)-R(ee)
beach la plage L(ah)   PL(ah)ZH
beautiful beau (m) B(O)   belle (f) B(e)L
beauty shop le salon de beauté
      L(uh)   S(ah)-L(O)ñ   D(uh)   B(O)-T(A)
bed le lit L(uh)   L(ee)
beef le boeuf L(uh)   B(ou)F
beer la bière L(ah)   B(ee)-(e)R
bellman le chasseur L(uh)   SH(ah)-S(ou)R
belt la ceinture L(ah)   S(ah)ñ-T(ou)R
big grand (m) GR(ah)ñ   grande (f) GR(ah)ND
bill l'addition (f) L(ah)-D(ee)-S(ee)-(O)ñ
black noir NW(ah)R
blanket la couverture L(ah)   K(oo)-V(e)R-T(ou)R
blue bleu BL(ou)
boat Le bateau L(uh)   B(ah)-T(O)
book Le livre L(uh)   L(ee)-VR(uh)
book store la librairie L(ah)   L(ee)-BR(e)-R(ee)
border la frontière L(ah)   FR(O)ñ-T(ee)-(e)R
boy le garçon L(uh)   G(ah)R-S(O)ñ
bracelet le bracelet L(uh)   BR(ah)-S(uh)-L(A)
brake le frein L(uh)   FR(ah)ñ
bread le pain L(uh)   P(ah)ñ
breakfast le petit déjeuner L(uh)   P(uh)-T(ee)   D(A)-ZH(ou)-N(A)

broiled grillé (f) GR☉-Y☉

brown brun (m) BR☉ñ brune (f) BR☉N

brush la brosse L☉ BR☉S

building le bâtiment L☉ B☉-T☉-M☉ñ

bus l'autobus (m) L☉-T☉-B☉S

bus station la gare routière L☉ G☉R R☉-T☉-☉R

bus stop l'arrêt de bus (m) L☉-R☉ D☉ B☉S

business l'affaires (f) L☉-F☉R

butter le beurre L☉ B☉R

buy (to) acheter ☉SH-T☉

C

cab le taxi L☉ T☉K-S☉

call (to) appeler ☉-P☉-L☉

camera l'appareil-photo (m) L☉-P☉-R☉ F☉-T☉

candy le bonbon L☉ B☉ñ-B☉ñ

car la voiture L☉ VW☉-T☉R

carrot la carotte L☉ K☉-R☉T

castle le château L☉ SH☉-T☉

cathedral la cathédrale L☉ K☉-T☉-DR☉L

celebration la fête L☉ F☉T

center le centre L☉ S☉ñ-TR☉

cereal le céréale L☉ S☉-R☉-☉L

chair la chaise L☉ SH☉Z

champagne la champagne L☉ SH☉ñ-P☉N-Y☉

change, exact la monnaie précise
      L☉ M☉-N☉ PR☉-S☉S

change (money) la monnaie L☉ M☉-N☉

change (to) changer SH☉ñ-ZH☉

cheap bon marché B☉ñ M☉R-SH☉

check (restaurant bill) l'addition (f) L☉-D☉-S☉-☉ñ

cheers! à votre santé! ☉-V☉-TR☉ S☉ñ-T☉

cheese le fromage LＵＨ FRＯ-MＡＨZH
chicken le poulet LＵＨ PＯＯ-LＡ
child l'enfant LＡＨＮ-FＡＨＮ
chocolate (flavor) au chocolat Ｏ SHＯ-KＯ-LＡＨ
church l'église (f) LＡ-GLＥＥZ
cigar le cigare LＵＨ SＥＥ-GＡＨR
cigarette la cigarette LＡＨ SＥＥ-GＡＨ-RＥＴ
city la ville LＡＨ VＥＥL
clean propre PRＯ-PRＵＨ
close (to) fermer FＥＲR-MＡ
closed fermé FＥＲR-MＡ
clothes les vêtements (m) LＡ VＥＴT-MＡＨＮ
cocktail le cocktail LＵＨ KＡＨK-TＡL
coffee le café LＵＨ KＡＨ-FＡ
cold froid (m) FRWＡＨ   froide (f) FRWＡＨD
comb le peigne LＵＨ PＥＴ-NYＵＨ
come (to) venir VＵＨ-NＥＲR
company (business) la compagnie LＡＨ KＯＮ-PＡＨ-NYＥＥ
computer l'ordinateur LＯR-DＥＥ-NＡＨ-TＵＲR
concert le concert LＵＨ KＯＮ-SＥＴR
conference la conférance LＡＨ KＯＮ-FＡ-RＡＨＮS
conference room la salle de conférences
          LＡＨ SＡＨ DＵＨ KＯＮ-FＡ-RＡＨＮS
congratulations félicitations FＡ-LＥＥ-SＥＥ-TＡＨ-SＥＥ-ＯＮ
copy machine le copieur LＵＨ KＯ-PＥＥ-ＵＲR
corn le maïs LＵＨ MＡＨ-ＥＥ
cough syrup le sirop contre la toux
          LＵＨ SＥＥ-RＯ KＯＮ-TRＵＨ LＡＨ TＯＯ
cover charge le couvert LＵＨ KＯＯ-VＥＴR
crab le crabe LＵＨ KRＡＨB
cream la crème LＡＨ KRＥＴM

credit card la carte de crédit L@h K@hRT D@h KR@-D@@

cup la tasse L@h T@hS

customs la douane L@h DW@N

D

dance (to) danser D@hñ-S@

dangerous dangereux (m) D@hñ-ZH@h-R@u

    dangereuse (f) D@hñ-ZH@h-R@uS

date (calender) la date L@h D@hT

day le jour L@h ZH@@R

December décembre D@-S@hñ-BR@h

delicious délicieux (m) D@-L@@-S@@-@u

    délicieuse (f) D@-L@@-S@@-@uS

delighted enchanté @hñ-SH@hñ-T@

dentist le dentiste L@h D@hñ-T@@ST

deodorant le déodorant D@-O-DO-R@hñ

department store le grand magasin

    L@h GR@hñ M@h-G@h-Z@ñ

departure le départ L@h D@-P@hR

dessert le dessert L@h D@-S@R

detour le détour L@h D@-T@@R

diabetic diabétique D@@-@h-B@-T@@K

diarrhea la diarrhée L@h D@@-@h-R@

dictionary le dictionnaire L@h D@@K-S@@-O-N@R

dinner le dîner L@h D@@-N@

dining room la salle à manger

    L@h S@hL @h M@hñ-ZH@

direction la direction L@h D@@-R@K-S@@-Oñ

dirty sale S@hL

disabled handicapé H@hñ-D@@-K@h-P@

discount la remise L@h R@h-M@@Z

distance la distance L@ DEES-T@ñS
doctor le docteur L@ D@K-T@R
document le document L@ DO-Kew-M@ñ
dollar le dollar L@ DO-L@R
down descendre DE-S@ñ-DR@
downtown en ville @ñ VEEL
dress la robe L@ R@B
drink (to) boire BW@R
drive (to) conduire K@ñ-DWEER
drugstore la pharmacie L@ F@R-M@-SEE
dry cleaner la teinturerie L@ T@ñ-Tew-@-REE
duck le canard L@ K@-N@R

E

ear l'oreille L@-R@-Y@
ear drops les gouttes pour les oreilles (f)
    L@ G@T P@R L@ Z@-R@-Y@
early tôt T@
east l'est (m) L@ST
easy facile F@-SEEL
eat (to) manger M@ñ-ZH@
eggs l'oeuf L@
eggs, fried les oeufs sur le plat (m/pl)
    L@ Z@F S@R L@ PL@
eggs, scrambled les oeufs sur les brouillés (m/pl)
    L@ Z@F S@R L@ BREE-Y@
electricity l'électricité (f) L@-L@K-TREE-SEE-T@
elevator l'ascenseur (m) L@-S@ñ-S@R
embassy l'ambassade (f) L@ñ-B@-S@D
emergency l'urgence (f) L@R-ZH@ñS
English anglais (m) L@ñ-GL@
    anglaise (f) @ñ-GL@Z

enough! C'est assez! SⒶ TⓐH-SⒶ
entrance l'entrée (f) Lⓐñ-TRⒶ
envelope l'enveloppe (f) Lⓐñ-Vⓤh-LⓄP
evening la soirée Lⓐh SWⓐh-RⒶ
everything tout Tⓞⓞ
excellent excéllent (m) ⒺK-SⒶ-Lⓐñ
    excéllante (f) ⒺK-SⒶ-LⓐñT
excuse me pardon PⓐR-DⓄñ
exit la sortie Lⓐh SⓄR-Tⓔⓔ
expensive cher SHⒺR
eye le yeux Lⓤh Zⓔⓔ-Yⓞⓤ
eye drops les gouttes pour les yeux
    LⒶ GⓞⓞT PⓞⓞR LⒶ Zⓔⓔ-Yⓞⓤ

F

face le visage Lⓤh Vⓔⓔ-SⓐhZH
far loin LWⒶñ
fare (cost) le tarif Lⓤh Tⓐh-RⓔⓔF
fast rapide Rⓐh-PⓔⓔD
fax, fax machine le fax Lⓤh FⓐKS
February février FⒶ-VRⓔⓔ-Ⓐ
few peu de Pⓞⓤ Dⓤh
film (for a camera) la pellicule Lⓐh PⒺ-Lⓔⓔ-KⓔⓌL
film (movie) le cinéma Lⓤh Sⓔⓔ-NⒶ-Mⓐh
fine/ very well très bien TRⒶ Bⓔⓔ-Ⓐñ
fingernail l'ongle (m) LⓄñ-GLⓤh
finger le doigt Lⓤh DWⓐh
fire extinguisher l'extincteur (m) LⒺK-STⓐñK-TⓞⓤR
fire! Au feu! Ⓞ Fⓞⓤ
first premier (m) PRⒺM-YⒶ
    première (f) PRⒺM-YⒺR
fish le poisson Lⓤh PWⓐh-SⓄñ

fit (to) aller ⓐⓗ-Lⓐ

flight le vol Lⓤⓗ VⓄL

floor (story) l'étage (m) Lⓐ-TⓐⓗZH

florist shop le fleuriste Lⓤⓗ FLⓄⓊ-RⓔⒺST

flower la fleur Lⓐⓗ FLⓄⓊR

food la nourriture Lⓐⓗ NⓄⓄ-RⓔⒺ-TⓔⓌR

foot le pied Lⓤⓗ PYⓐ

fork la fourchette Lⓐⓗ FⓄⓄR-SHⒺT

France la France Lⓐⓗ FRⓐⓗñS

french fries les frites Lⓐ FRⓔⒺT

fresh frais FRⓐ

Friday vendredi Vⓐⓗñ-DRⓤⓗ-DⒺ

fried frit (m) FRⒺ frite (f) FRⒺT

friend l'ami (m) l'amie (f) Lⓐⓗ-MⒺ

fruit le fruit Lⓤⓗ FRWⒺ

funny drôle DRⓄL

G

gas station la station de service
    Lⓐⓗ STⓐⓗ-SⒺ-Ⓞñ Dⓤⓗ SⓔR-VⒺS

gasoline l'essence (f) LⒺ-SⓐⓗñS

gate la barriere Lⓐⓗ BⓐⓗR-Ⓔ-ⓔR

gentleman le monsieur Mⓤⓗ-SYⓄⓊ

gift le cadeau Lⓤⓗ Kⓐⓗ-DⓄ

girl la fille Lⓐⓗ FⒺ

glass (drinking) le verre Lⓤⓗ VⓔR

glasses (eye) les lunettes Lⓐ LⓔⓌ-NⒺT

glove le gant Lⓤⓗ Gⓐⓗñ

go (to) aller ⓐⓗ-Lⓐ

gold (mineral) l'or LⓄR

golf le golf Lⓤⓗ GⓄLF

golf course le terrain de golf Lⓤⓗ Tⓔ-Rⓐñ Dⓤⓗ GⓄLF

good bon (m) BOñ bonne (f) BuhN
goodbye au revoir O-Ruh-VWahR
goose L'oie LWah
grape le raisin Luh RA-Zañ
grateful reconnaissant Ruh-KO-Nē-Sahñ
gray gris (m) GRē grise (f) GRēS
green vert (m) VēR verte (f) VēRT
grocery store l'épicerie (f) LA-Pē-Sē-Rē
group le groupe Luh GRooP
guide le guide Luh GēD
H
hair les cheveux (m,p) LA SHuh-Vou
hairbrush la brosse à cheveux
    Lah BROS ah SHuh-Vou
haircut la coupe de cheveux Lah KooP Duh SHuh-Vou
ham le jambon Luh ZHahñ-BOñ
hamburger le hamburger Luh ahM-BēR-GēR
hand la main Lah Mañ
happy heureux (m) ou-Rouou heureuse (f) ou-RouS
have, I jai ZHA
he il ēL
head la tête Lah TēT
headache mal a la tete Mah Lah Lah TēT
health club le centre sportif
    Luh Sahñ-TRuh SPOR-TēF
heart condition mal au coeur Mah LO-Kour
heart le coeur Luh Kour
heat la chaleur Lah SHah-Lour
hello bonjour BOñ-ZHooR
help! au secours! O Suh-KooR
here ici ē-Sē

holiday la fête L@h F@T
hospital l'hôpital (m) L@-P@@-T@hL
hot dog le hot dog L@h H@hT D@G
hotel l'hôtel (m) L@-T@L
hour l'heure L@R
how comment K@-M@ñ
hurry (to) depecher D@-P@@-SH@
hurry! dépechez-vous D@-P@@-SH@ V@@
I
I Je ZH@h
ice la glace L@h GL@S
ice cream la glace L@h GL@S
ice cubes les glaçons (f) L@ GL@h-S@ñ
ill malade M@h-L@hD
important important (m) @ñ-P@R-T@hñ
         importante (f) @ñ-P@R-T@hñT
indigestion la dyspepsie L@h D@@S-P@P-S@@
information les renseignements (m)
         L@ R@hñ-S@N-Y@h-M@hñ
inn l'auberge (f) L@-B@RZH
interpreter l'interprète (m) L@ñ-T@R-PR@T
J
jacket le veston L@h V@S-T@ñ
jam la confiture L@h K@ñ-F@@-T@wR
January janvier ZH@hñ-V@@-@
jewelry les bijoux (m) L@ B@@-ZH@@
jewelry store la bijouterie L@ B@@-ZH@@-T@-R@@
job le travail L@h TR@h-V@h-Y@@
juice le jus L@h ZH@@
July juillet ZH@@-@@-@
June juin ZH@@-@ñ

K

ketchup le ketchup Lⓤ Kⓔ-CHⓤP

key la clé Lⓐ KLⒶ

kiss le baiser Lⓤ BⒶ-SⒶ

knife le couteau Lⓤ Kⓞⓞ-Tⓞ

know, I je sais ZHⓤ   SⒶ

L

ladies' restroom Dames DⓐM

lady la dame Lⓐ DⓐM

lamb l'agneau Lⓐñ-Yⓞ

language la langue Lⓐ LⓐNG

large grand (m) GRⓐñ grande (f) GRⓐND

late tard TⓐR

laundry la blanchisserie Lⓤ BLⓐñ-SHⒺ-Sⓔ-Rⓔ

lawyer l'avocat (m) Lⓐ-Vⓞ-Kⓐ

left (direction) à gauche (f) ⓐ GⓞSH

leg la jambe Lⓤ ZHⓐñB

lemon le citron Lⓤ Sⓔ-TRⓞñ

less moins MWⓐñ

letter la lettre Lⓐ Lⓔ-TRⓤ

lettuce la laitue Lⓐ LⒶ-Tⓔⓦ

light la lumière Lⓐ LⓔⓦM-YⓔR

like comme KⓞM

like, I je veux ZHⓤ Vⓞⓞ

like, I would je voudrais ZHⓤ Vⓞⓞ-DRⒶ

lip la lèvre Lⓐ Lⓔ-VRⓤ

lipstick le rouge Lⓤ RⓞⓞZH

little (amount) un peu ⓤñ Pⓞⓤ

little (size) petit (m) Pⓤ-Tⓔ petite (f) Pⓤ-TⓔT

live (to) vivre Vⓔ-VRⓤ

lobster le homard Lⓞ-MⓐR

long long (m) LⓄñ longue (f) LⓄNG
lost perdu PⒺR-Dⓔⓦ
love l'amour Lⓐⱨ-MⓄⓄR
luck la chance Lⓐⱨ SHⓐⱨñS
luggage les bagages (m) LⒶ Bⓐⱨ-GⓐⱨZH
lunch le déjeuner Lⓤⱨ DⒶ-ZHⓄⓤ-NⒶ
M
maid la domestique Lⓐⱨ DⓄM-ⒺS-TⒺK
mail le courrier Lⓤⱨ KⓄⓄ-RⒺⒺ-Ⓐ
makeup le maquillage Lⓤⱨ Mⓐⱨ-KⒺⒺ-YⓐⱨZH
man l'homme (m) LⓄM
manager le gérant Lⓤⱨ ZHⒶ-Rⓐⱨñ
map le plan Lⓤⱨ PLⓐⱨñ
March mars MⓐⱨRS
market le marché Lⓤⱨ MⓐⱨR-SHⒶ
match (light) l'allumette (f) Lⓐⱨ-Lⓔⓦ-MⒺT
May mai MⒶ
mayonnaise la mayonnaise Lⓐⱨ Mⓐⱨ-YⓄ-NⒺZ
meal le repas Rⓤⱨ-Pⓐⱨ
meat la viande Lⓐⱨ VⒺⒺ-ⓐⱨñD
mechanic le mécanicien Lⓤⱨ MⒶ-Kⓐⱨ-NⒺⒺ-SⒺⒺ-ⓐⱨñ
medicine le médecine Lⓤⱨ MⒶ-Dⓐⱨ-SⒺⒺN
meeting le rendez-vous Lⓤⱨ Rⓐⱨñ-DⒶ-VⓄⓄ
mens' restroom messieurs MⒺ-SYⓄⓤ
menu la carte Lⓐⱨ KⓐⱨRT
message le message Lⓤⱨ MⒺ-Sⓐⱨ-ZH
milk le lait Lⓤⱨ LⒶ
mineral water l'eau minérale (f) LⓄ MⒺⒺ-NⒶ-RⓐⱨL
minute le minute Lⓤⱨ MⒺⒺ-NⓔⓦT
Miss mademoiselle MⓐⱨD-MWⓐⱨ-ZⒺL
mistake la faute Lⓐⱨ FⓄT

misunderstanding le malentendu
   LUH MAL-ahn-Tahn-DEW

moment le moment LUH MO-Mahn

Monday lundi LUHN-DEE

money l'argent (m) LAHR-ZHahn

month le mois LUH MWah

monument le monument LUH MO-New-Mahn

more plus PLEW

morning le matin LUH Mah-Tahn

mosque la mosquée LAH MOS-KA

mother la mère LAH MeR

mountain la montagne LAH MOhn-Tahn-YUH

movies le cinéma LUH SEE-NA-Mah

Mr. monsieur MUH-SYOO

Mrs. madame Mah-DahM

much, too trop TRO

museum le musée LUH Mew-ZA

mushroom le champignon LUH SHahn-PEEN-YON

music la musique LAH Mew-ZEEK

mustard la moutarde LAH Moo-TARD

N

nail polish la vernis à ongles
   LAH VeR-NEE Sah Ohn-GLUH

name le nom LUH NOhn

napkin la serviette LAH SeR-VEE-eT

napkins (sanitary) la serviette hygiénique (f)
   LAH SeR-VEE-eT EE-ZHEE-A-NeeK

near près de PRA DUH

neck le cou LUH Koo

need, I j'ai besoin ZHA BUH-ZWahn

never jamais ZHah-MA

newspaper le journal L_{uh} ZHOOR-NahL

newstand le kiosque L_{uh} KEE-ahSK

next time la prochaine Lah PRO-SHāñ

night la nuit Lah NWEE

nightclub la boite de nuit Lah BWahT D_{uh} NWEE

no non NOñ

no smoking non fumeurs NOñ FEW-MouR

noon midi MEE-DEE

north le nord L_{uh} NOR

notary le notaire L_{uh} NO-TēR

November novembre NO-Vahñ-BR_{uh}

now maintenant Mâñ-T_{uh}-Nahñ

number le numéro L_{uh} New-MA-RO

nurse l'infirmière (f) Lâñ-FEER-MEE-êR

O

occupied occupé O-Kew-PA

ocean l'océan (m) LO-SA-ahñ

October octobre OK-TO-BR_{uh}

officer l'officier (m) LO-FEE-SEE-A

oil l'huile (f) Lew-EEL

omelet l'omelette (f) LOM-LêT

one way (traffic) sens unique SahñS ew-NEEK

onion le oignon L_{uh} ZO-NYOñ

open (to) ouvrir oo-VREER

opera l'opéra (m) LO-PA-Rah

operator le standardiste L_{uh} STahN-DahR-DEEST

optician l'opticien LOP-TEE-SEE-âñ

orange (color) orange O-RahñZH

orange (fruit) l'orange (f) LO-RahñZH

order (to) commander KO-Mahñ-DA

original original O-REE-ZHEE-NahL

owner le propriétaire L⒲ PR⓪-PR⒠-Y⒠-T⒠R
oysters les huîtres (f/p) L⒜ W⒠-TR⒲
P
package le paquet L⒲ P⒜-K⒠
paid payé P⒜-Y⒜
pain la douleur L⒜ D⓪⓪-L⒴R
painting la peinture L⒜ P⒜ñ-T⒲R
pantyhose les collants
paper le papier L⒲ P⒜-P⒠-⒜
park le parc L⒲ P⒜RK
park (to) stationner ST⒜-S⒠-⓪-N⒜
partner (business) associé ⒜-S⓪-S⒠-⒜
party la soirée L⒜ SW⒜-R⒜
passenger le passager L⒲ P⒜-S⒜-ZH⒜
passport le passeport L⒲ P⒜S-P⓪R
pasta les pâtés L⒜ P⒜-T⒜
pastry la patrisserie L⒜ P⒜-T⒠-S⒲-R⒠
pen le stylo L⒲ ST⒠-L⓪
pencil le crayon L⒲ KR⒜-Y⓪ñ
pepper le poivre L⒲ PW⒜-VR⒲
perfume le parfum L⒲ P⒜R-F⒲ñ
person la personne L⒜ P⒠R-S⓪N
person to person de communication avec préavis
    D⒲ K⓪-M⒠w-N⒠-K⒜-S⒠-⓪ñ ⒜-V⒠K PR⒜-⒜-V⒠
pharmacist le pharmacien D⒠wN F⒜R-M⒜-S⒠-⒜ñ
pharmacy la pharmacie L⒜ F⒜R-M⒜-S⒠
phone book l'annuaire L⒜-N⒠w-⒠R
photo la photo L⒜ F⓪-T⓪
photographer le photographier L⒲ F⓪-T⓪-GR⒜-F⒠-⒜
pie la tarte L⒜ T⒜RT
pillow l'oreiller (m) L⓪-R⒜-Y⒜

pink rose R(o)Z

pizza la pizza L(ah) P(ee)D-S(ah)

plastic le plastique L(uh) PL(ah)S-T(ee)K

plate l'assiette (f) L(ah)-S(ee)-(ê)T

please s'il vous plaît S(ee)L V(oo) PL(ê)

pleasure le plaisir L(uh) PL(ê)-Z(ee)R

police le police L(uh) P(o)-L(ee)S

police station la poste de police
    L(ah) P(o)ST D(uh) P(uh)-L(ee)S

pork le porc L(uh) P(o)RK

porter le porteur L(uh) P(o)R-T(uh)R

post office la poste L(ah) P(o)ST

postcard la carte postale L(ah) K(ah)RT P(o)S-T(ah)L

potato la pomme de terre L(ah) P(uh)M D(uh) T(ê)R

pregnant enceinte (ah)ñ-S(ã)ñT

prescription la prescription PR(ê)-SKR(ee)P-S(ee)-(o)ñ

price le prix L(uh) PR(ee)

problem le problème L(uh) PR(o)-BL(ê)M

profession la profession L(ah) PR(o)-F(ê)-S(ee)-(o)N

public publique P(ew)B-L(ee)K

public telephone le téléphone public
    L(uh) T(a)-L(a)-F(o)N P(ew)-BL(ee)K

purified purifié P(ew)R-(ee)-F(ee)-(a)

purple violet (m) V(ee)-(o)-L(a) violette (f) V(ee)-(o)-L(ê)T

purse le sac L(uh) S(ah)K

Q

quality la qualité L(ah) K(ah)-L(ee)-T(a)

question la question L(ah) K(ê)S-T(ee)-(o)ñ

quickly rapidement R(ah)-P(ee)D-M(ah)ñ

quiet!, be taisez-vous T(a)-Z(a) V(oo)

quiet tranquille TRⓐñ-KⓔL

R

radio la radio Lⓐ RⓐD-YⓄ

railroad le chemin de fer Lⓤ SHⓤ-Mⓐñ Dⓤ FⓔR

rain la pluie Lⓐ PLⓔw-ⓔ

raincoat l'imperméable (m) Lⓐñ-PⓔR-MⒶ-ⓐB-Lⓤ

ramp la rampe Lⓐ RⓐMP

rare (cooked) saignant SⒶ-NYⓐñ

razor blades les lames de rasoir
    LⒶ LⓐM Dⓤ Rⓐ-SWⓐR

ready prêt PRⓔ

receipt le reçu Lⓤ Rⓤ-Sⓔw

recommend (to) recommender Rⓤ-KⓄ-Mⓐñ-DⒶ

red rouge RⓄZH

repeat! répéter! RⒶ-PⒶ-TⒶ

reservation la réservation Lⓐ RⒶ-ZⓔR-Vⓐ-Sⓔ-Ⓞñ

restaurant le restaurant Lⓤ RⓔS-TⓄ-Rⓐñ

return revenir Rⓤ-Vⓤ-NⓔR

rice le riz Lⓤ Rⓔ

rich riche RⓔSH

right (correct) correct KⓄ-RⓔKT

right (direction) à droite ⓐ DRWⓐT

road le chemin Lⓤ SHⓤ-Mⓐñ

room la chambre Lⓐ SHⓐñ-BRⓤ

round trip l'aller et retour Lⓐ-LⒶ Ⓐ Rⓤ-TⓄR

S

safe (in a hotel) le coffre-fort Lⓤ KⓄ-FRⓤ FⓄR

salad la salade Lⓐ Sⓐ-LⓐD

sale la vente Lⓐ VⓐñT

salmon le saumon Lⓤ SⓄ-MⓄñ

salt le sel Lⓤ SⓔL

sandwich le sandwich Luh   Sahn-WEECH

Saturday samedi Sah-Muh-DEE

scissors les ciseaux (m) LA SEE-ZO

sculpture la sculpture Lah SKEWLP-TewR

seafood les fruits de mer (m) LA FRWEE Duh MER

season la saison Lah SE-ZOñ

seat la place Lah PLahS

secretary le secrétaire Luh SE-KRA-TER

section la section Lah   SEK-SEE-ooñ

September septembre SEP-Tahñ-BRuh

service le service Luh SER-VEES

several plusieurs PLew-ZYuR

shampoo le shampooing Luh SHahñ-Poo-EEN

sheets, bed les draps LA DRahP

shirt la chemise Lah SHuh-MEES

shoe la chaussure Lah SHO-SewR

shoe store la boutique de chaussures
     Luh Boo-TEEK Duh SHO-SewR

shop la boutique Lah Boo-TEEK

shopping center le centre commercial
     Luh Sahñ-TRuh KO-MER-SEE-ahL

shower la douche Lah DooSH

shrimp les crevettes LA KRuh-VET

sick malade Mah-LahD

sign (display) le signe Luh SEEN-Yuh

signature la signature Lah SEEN-Yah-TuhR

silence! silence SEE-LahñS

single seul SuuL

sir monsieur Muh-SYou

sister la soeur Lah SuuR

size la taille Lah TA-You

skin la peau Lⓐ Pⓞ

skirt la jupe Lⓐⓗ ZHⓞⓞP

sleeve la manche Lⓐⓗ MⓐⓗñSH

slowly lentement Lⓐⓗñ-Tⓤⓗ-Mⓐⓗñ

small (amount) un peu ⓤⓗñ Pⓞⓤ

small (size) petit (m) Pⓤⓗ-Tⓔⓔ   petite (F) Pⓤⓗ-TⓔⓔT

smile (to) sourire Sⓞⓞ-RⓔⓔR

smoke (to) fumer Fⓔⓦ-Mⓐ

soap le savon Lⓤⓗ Sⓐⓗ-Vⓞñ

sock les chaussettes Lⓐ SHⓞ-SⓔT

some quelque KⓔL-Kⓤⓗ

something quelque chose KⓔL-Kⓤⓗ SHⓞZ

sometimes quelquefois KⓔL-Kⓤⓗ-FWⓐⓗ

soon bientôt Bⓔⓔ-ⓐñ-Tⓞ

sorry, I am Je suis désolé ZHⓤⓗ SWⓔⓔ Dⓐ-Sⓞ-Lⓐ

soup la soupe Lⓐⓗ SⓞⓞP

south le sud Lⓤⓗ SⓔⓦD

souvenir le souvenir Lⓤⓗ Sⓞⓞ-Vⓤⓗ-NⓔⓔR

speciality la spécialité Lⓐⓗ SPⓐ-Sⓔⓔ-ⓐⓗ-Lⓔⓔ-Tⓐ

speed la vitesse Lⓐⓗ Vⓔⓔ-TⓔS

spoon la cuillère Lⓐⓗ KWⓔⓔ-ⓔR

sport le sport Lⓤⓗ SPⓞR

spring (season) le printemps Lⓤⓗ PRⓐñ-Tⓐⓗñ

stairs les escaliers Lⓐ Zⓔ-SKⓐⓗL-Yⓐ

stamp le timbre Lⓤⓗ Tⓐñ-BRⓤⓗ

station la gare Lⓐⓗ GⓐⓗR

steak le bifteck Lⓤⓗ BⓔⓔF-TⓔK

steamed a l'etuvée ⓐⓗ Lⓐ-Tⓔⓦ-Vⓐ

stop! arrêtez ⓐⓗ-Rⓔ-Tⓐ

store le magasin Lⓤⓗ Mⓐⓗ-Gⓐⓗ-Zⓐñ

storm la tempête Lⓐⓗ Tⓐⓗñ-PⓔT

straight ahead tout droit T⑩ DRW⒜

strawberry la fraise L⒜ FR⒠Z

street la rue L⒜ R⒠

string la ficelle L⒜ F⒠-S⒠L

subway le métro L⒰ M⒜-TR⑩

sugar le sucre L⒰ S⒠-KR⒰

suit (clothes) le complet L⒰ K⑩ñ-PL⒠

suitcase la valise L⒜ V⒜-L⒠S

summer l'été L⒜-T⒜

sun le soleil L⒰ S⑩-L⒜

sun tan lotion la lotion à bronzer
　　　L⒜ L⑩-S⒠-⑩ñ ⒜ BR⑩ñ-Z⒜

Sunday dimanche D⒠-M⒜ñSH

sunglasses les lunettes de soleil (f)
　　　L⒜ L⒠-N⒠T D⒰ S⑩-L⒜

supermarket le supermarché
　　　L⒰ S⒠-P⒠R-M⒜R-SH⒜

surprise la surprise L⒜ S⒠R-PR⒠Z

sweet doux D⑩

swim (to) nager N⒜-ZH⒜

swimming pool la piscine L⒜ P⒠-S⒠N

synagogue la synagogue L⒜ S⒠-N⒜-G⑩G

T

table la table L⒜ T⒜-BL⒰

tampons les tampons L⒜ T⒜ñ-P⑩ñ

tape (sticky) le ruban L⒰ R⒠-B⒜ñ

tape recorder le magnétophone L⒰ M⒜G-N⒜-T⑩-F⑩N

tax la taxe L⒜ T⒜KS

taxi le taxi L⒰ T⒜K-S⒠

tea le thé L⒰ T⒜

telegram le télégramme L⒰ T⒜-L⒜-GR⒜M

telephone le téléphone L⒰ T⒜-L⒜-F⒪N
television la télévision L⒜ T⒜-L⒜-V㋍-S㋍-O⒩
temperature la température L⒰ T⒜⒩-P㋍-R⒜-T⒠R
temple le temple L⒰ T⒜⒩-PL⒰
tennis la tennis L⒜ T㋍-N㋍S
tennis court le terrain de tennis
    L⒰ T㋍-R⒜⒩ D⒰ T㋍-N㋍S
thank you merci M㋍R-S㋍
that cela S⒰-L⒜
the le (m)L⒰ la (f) L⒜
theater le théâtre L⒰ T⒜-⒜-TR⒰
there la L⒜
they ils ㋍L
this ce/cet/cette S⒰ / S㋍T / S㋍T
thread le fil L⒰ F㋍L
throat la gorge L⒜ GORZH
Thursday jeudi ZH⒪-D㋍
ticket le billet L⒰ B㋍-Y⒜
tie la cravate L⒜ KR⒜-V⒜T
time l'heure L⒪R
tip (gratuity) le pourboire L⒰ P⒪R-BW⒜R
tire (car) le pneu L⒰ P⒰-N⒪
tired fatigue F⒜-T㋍-G⒜
toast pan grillé P⒜⒩ GR㋍-Y⒜
tobacco le tabac L⒰ T⒜-B⒜K
today aujourd'hui ⒪H-ZH⒪R-DW㋍
toe l'orteil LOR-T⒜
together ensemble ⒜⒩-S⒜⒩-BL⒰
toilet la toilette L⒜ TW⒜-L㋍T
toilet paper le papier hygiénique
    L⒰ P⒜-P㋍-⒜ ㋍-ZH㋍-⒜-N㋍K

tomato la tomate L@h TO-M@hT

tomorrow demain D@h-M@ñ

tooth ache le mal aux dents L@h M@hL O D@hñ

toothbrush la brosse à dents L@h BROS @h D@hñ

toothpaste le dentifrice L@h D@hñ-TEE-FREES

toothpick le cure-dents L@h KewR D@hñ

tour le visite L@h VEE-ZEET

tourist le touriste L@h Too-REEST

tourist office le bureau de tourisme
    L@h Bew-RO D@h Too-REES-M@h

towel la serviette L@h SëR-VEE-@hT

train le train L@h TR@hñ

travel agency l'agence de voyage
    L@h-ZH@hñS D@h VW@h-Y@hZH

travelers check le chèque de voyage
    L@h SH@hK D@h VW@h-Y@hZH

trip le voyage L@h VW@h-Y@hZH

trousers le pantalon L@h P@hñ-T@h-LOñ

trout la truite L@h TRW@ew-EET

truth la vérité L@h VA-REE-TA

Tuesday mardi M@hR-DEE

turkey le dinde L@h D@hñND

U

umbrella la parapluie L@h P@h-R@h-PL@ew-EE

understand (to) comprendre KON-PR@hñ-DR@h

underwear les sous-vêtements LA Soo V@hT-M@hñ

United States les Etats-Unis LA ZA-T@h-Zew-NEE

university l'université (f) L@ew-NEE-VëR-SEE-TA

up haut O

urgent urgent @uR-ZH@hñ

V

vacancies (accommodation) chambres libres (f)
SH@ñ-BR⑩ L⒠-BR⑩

vacant libre L⒠-BR⑩

vacation les vacances L④ V@-K@ñS

valuable précieux (m) PR④-SY⑩
précieuse (f) PR④-SY⑩S

value le valeur L⑩ V@-L⑩R

vanilla la vanille L@ V@-N⒠L

veal le veau L⑩ V⑩

vegetables les légumes (m) L④ L④-G⑩M

view la vue L@ V⑩

vinegar le vinaigre L⑩ V⒠-N④-GR⑩

voyage le voyage L⑩ VW@-Y@ZH

W

wait! attendez @-T@ñ-D④

waiter le garçon L⑩ G@R-S⑩ñ

waitress la serveuse L@ S⒠R-V⑩S

want, I Je voudrais ZH⑩ V⑩-DR④

wash (to) laver L@-V④

watch (time piece) la montre L@ M⑩ñ-TR⑩

watch out! attention @-T@ñ-S⒠-⑩ñ

water l'eau L⑩

watermelon le pastèque L⑩ P@S-T⒠K

we nous N⑩

weather le temps L⑩ T@ñ

Wednesday mercredi M⒠R-KR⑩-D⒠

week la semaine L@ S@-M⒠N

weekend le week-end L⑩ W⒠K-⒠ND

welcome bienvenu B⒠-@ñ-V⒠-N⑩

well done (cooked) bien cuit B⒠-@ñ KW⒠

west l'ouest L⊕⊕-ⓔST

what? que? / quoi? Kⓤⱨ / KWⓐⱨ

wheelchair le fauteuil roulant
    Lⓤⱨ Fⓞ-Tⓞⱥ-Yⓞⱥ Rⓞⓞ-Lⓐⱨñ

when quand Kⓐⱨñ

where ou ⓞⓞ

which quel / quelle KⓔL

white blanc (m) BLⓐⱨñK blanche (f) BLⓐⱨñSH

who qui Kⓔⓔ

why? pourquoi? PⓞⓞR-KWⓐⱨ

wife la femme Lⓐⱨ FⓐⱨM

wind le vent Lⓤⱨ Vⓐⱨñ

window la fenêtre Lⓐⱨ Fⓤⱨ-Nⓔ-TRⓤⱨ

wine le vin Lⓤⱨ Vⓐñ

wine list la carte de vins Lⓐⱨ KⓐⱨRT Dⓤⱨ Vⓐñ

winter l'hiver Lⓔⓔ-VⓔR

with avec ⓐⱨ-VⓔK

woman la femme Lⓐⱨ FⓐⱨM

wonderful merveilleux MⓔR-Vⓐ-Yⓞⱥ

world le monde Lⓤⱨ MⓞñD

wrong avoir tort   ⓐⱨ-VWⓐⱨR TⓞR

XYZ

year l'année Lⓐⱨ-Nⓐ

yellow jaune ZHⓞN

yes oui Wⓔⓔ

yesterday hier YⓔR

you tu / vous Tⓔⱥ / Vⓞⓞ

zipper la fermeture Lⓐⱨ FⓔR-Mⓤⱨ-TⓔⱥR

zoo le zoo Lⓤⱨ Zⓞ

INDEX

EPLS VOWEL SYMBOLS

(A)	(ă)	(ah)
Ace	Cat	Rock
Bake	Sad	Hot
Safe	Hat	Off

(EE)	(ĕ)	(ew)
See	Men	New
Green	Red	Few
Feet	Bed	Dew

(O)	(oo)	(ou)
Oak	Cool	Could
Cold	Pool	Would
Phone	Too	Cook

(uh)
Up
Sun
Run

FRENCH 1/95